ideaSPOTTING

ideaSPOTTING

HOW TO FIND YOUR NEXT GREAT IDEA

Sam Harrison

MacHillock Publishing
ATLANTA, GEORGIA

15 14 13 12 11 8 7 6 5 4

ISBN: 978-0-9744996-5-9

Library of Congress Control Number: 2005033311

Library of Congress Cataloging-in-Publication Data
Available from Library of Congress

For more information, visit
www.zingzone.com

Sam Harrison has more than twenty years of experience in creative agency, corporate and consulting roles. He was senior vice president of creative services and branding for an S&P 500 firm and has worked with such clients and associates as the NFL, Major League Baseball, Hallmark, Hasbro, Merrill Lynch and John Denver Environmental Groups.

Sam is an in-demand speaker who provides keynotes and workshops to organizations, conferences and conventions throughout North America. He also teaches creativity, writing and presentation skills classes at a graduate studies program for brand communicators.

He is the author of two other books: *IdeaSelling: Successfully pitch your creative ideas to bosses, clients and other decision makers* and *ZING! Five steps and 101 tips for creativity on command.* And he is a frequent contributor to *HOW Design, Fast Company* and other magazines, blogs and websites.

He can be reached at www.zingzone.com.

For Hope.

table
OF CONTENTS

be an IdeaSpotter.

NOT A TRAINSPOTTER.

"Trainspotter" is British slang for a dull, obsessive guy whose hobby is standing for hours on station platforms, meticulously recording the serial numbers of train cars passing by.

If the British call you a trainspotter, they're likely calling you a loser.

IdeaSpotters, on the other hand, are surefire winners. The only thing they have in common with trainspotters is a predilection for notebooks.

Rather than record engine numbers, IdeaSpotters capture ideas. Lots of ideas. And you won't see IdeaSpotters planted on platforms, patiently waiting for these ideas to appear. Truth is, they don't stand any place for very long.

IdeaSpotters are over here one day, over there the next. Exploring new places. Making new connections. Uncovering new insights.

This little book puts you in touch with IdeaSpotters—designers and writers, artists and illustrators, marketers and salespeople, CEOs and diplomats, scientists and inventors, event planners and product developers, athletes and actors, chefs and musicians, philosophers and educators. And dozens of other creative folks.

Succinct examples and quick exercises help you discover the secrets and techniques of IdeaSpotters. You'll learn how they've explored life and made associations. You'll see how and where they've found great ideas.

SO HERE ARE YOUR CHOICES.

You can drift toward becoming the trainspotting type by sitting where you're sitting, doing what you're doing and getting what you're getting.

Or you can start becoming an IdeaSpotter by climbing aboard. Because this train is leaving the station.

1

NOBODY SPOTS
hot ideas in cold offices.

SO WHY SIT THERE?

ideaSPOTTING
= EXPLORATION + ASSOCIATION

EXPLORE.

LOOK BEYOND THE OBVIOUS AND OBLIGATORY.

Uncover new territory. Discover new thoughts.
Dive in. *Dig deep.*

"We must go beyond textbooks,
go out into the bypaths
and untrodden depths of the wilderness
and travel and explore and tell the world
the glories of our journey."

—John Hope Franklin, HISTORIAN

"Exploration is the essence
of the human spirit."

—Frank Borman, ASTRONAUT

"In wisdom gathered over time, I found that
every experience is a form of
exploration."

—Ansel Adams, PHOTOGRAPHER

"Gather and pass on what comes from the depths."

—Paul Klee, ARTIST

Klee compared creative people to trees, extending roots of perception to draw in the nourishment of experience. Nutrition flows through trunks and branches, sprouting ideas.

ASSOCIATE.

CONNECT DOTS. BUILD BRIDGES.
SPARK CHAIN REACTIONS.
AMALGAMATE. ALCHEMIZE.

"Creativity is the power to connect the
seemingly unconnected."

—William Plomer, AUTHOR

"When we try to pick out anything by itself,
we find it hitched to everything else in the
universe."

—John Muir, NATURALIST

"The web of our life is of a mingled yarn..."

—William Shakespeare

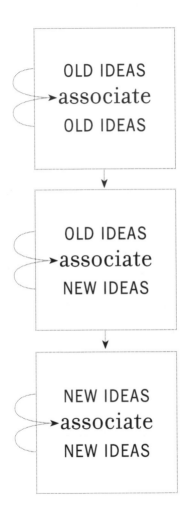

BUT WHY explore WHEN THE FACTS ARE BEFORE YOU?

There's nothing wrong with backbone data. Or raw statistics. Or bedrock demographics. They're fine as far as they go.

The problem is, they don't go far enough. Not if you're looking for information instead of data. And insights instead of information.

IN-FORM OR IN-SIGHT?

To spot ideas, you want insights. Lots of them. Because ideas aren't spotted in forms. They're spotted in sights—those revelatory insights seized only when you roam new turfs, meet new people and have new experiences.

LIGHT BULBS WEREN'T INVENTED BY EXPLORING CANDLES.

IRON SHIPS WEREN'T MADE BY EXPLORING WOOD BOATS.

SKYSCRAPERS WEREN'T DESIGNED BY EXPLORING BUNGALOWS.

WALKMANS WEREN'T INVENTED BY EXPLORING TURNTABLES.

CELL PHONES WEREN'T CONCEIVED BY EXPLORING LAND LINES.

MACS WEREN'T DESIGNED BY EXPLORING CLUNKY, DULL PCS.

TO GET PAST WHAT'S STIFLING YOU, MOVE BEYOND WHAT'S STARING YOU IN THE FACE.

It's tough to get a new slant on something when you're looking at it head-on.

A cube head-on is a square.
Step left or right and see its full dimensions.

"People don't think carrot cake is weird.
So when I serve a parsnip cake, that's not
weird to me. It's just one step to the side."

—Marcus Samuelsson, NEW YORK CHEF

EXPLORING IGNITES THE
idea PROCESS.

My book *Zing! Five steps and 101 tips for creativity on command* focuses on a five-step methodology for generating ideas. Here's how the process looks:

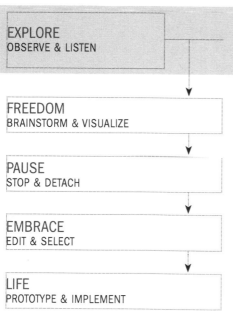

EXPLORE
OBSERVE & LISTEN

↓

FREEDOM
BRAINSTORM & VISUALIZE

↓

PAUSE
STOP & DETACH

↓

EMBRACE
EDIT & SELECT

↓

LIFE
PROTOTYPE & IMPLEMENT

IdeaSpotting focuses on the Explore phase of the creative process—using exploration and association to spot great ideas!

There's no formula for creativity. No cookie-cutter solution.

BUT THERE IS DEFINITELY A FLOWING FORM IN THE WAY HIGHLY CREATIVE PEOPLE GLIDE TOWARD EXCITING, ENDLESS IDEAS.

"Behind every design is a process—a thought process. And that process transcends design itself. If you are mapping out a sales strategy, or streamlining a manufacturing operation, or crafting a new system for innovating—if you work in the world of business—you are engaged in the practice of design."

—Chris Bangle, DESIGN DIRECTOR, BMW

idea**SPOTTING BEGINS WITH EXPLORING.**
exploring begins with an open mind.

It's impossible for people to learn what they think they already know, said Epictetus.

And filmmaker Clint Eastwood put it this way: "Once you feel you know everything, you're done. You're either repetitive or boring or both."

Ideas are as rare as ivory-billed woodpeckers when the mind is closed.

START WITH A BLANK SLATE.
FILL IT WITH INSIGHTS.

When it's open, IdeaSpotting happens. You then have what philosopher John Locke termed *tabula rasa*, a "soft tablet" or blank slate.

All valid knowledge, argued Locke, comes through experience.

"No man's knowledge can go beyond his experiences."

—John Locke, PHILOSOPHER

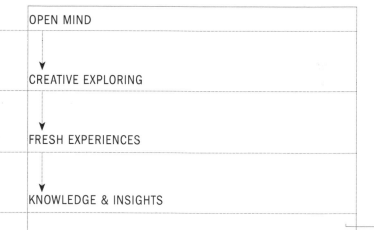

OPEN MIND

CREATIVE EXPLORING

FRESH EXPERIENCES

KNOWLEDGE & INSIGHTS

"You have brains in your head,
you have feet in your shoes.
You can steer yourself
any direction you choose…

Out there things can happen
and frequently do
to people as brainy
and footsy as you"

—Dr. Seuss,
 Oh, the Places You'll Go

open your mind

AND PEOPLE WILL SHOW YOU WHAT'S ON THEIR MINDS.

For years, soft-drink customers lugged twelve-packs built like suitcases. This beat juggling six-packs, but the bulky box was a pain to store in refrigerators.

Alcoa wanted a better idea. So its people spent days in supermarkets, watching customers select and tote soft drinks. They then went home with customers to see how they stored and consumed the drinks.

Alcoa explorers saw people place a few cans in the refrigerator and stash the carton with remaining cans in the pantry. When cold soft drinks were gone, consumers usually searched the fridge for another type of drink rather than return to the pantry.

In other words, the suitcase box was actually inhibiting the use of soft-drink cans. Bad news if you're a can manufacturer.

Alcoa explorers hauled their insights into brainstorming sessions and generated hundreds of ideas. The result was Fridge Pack, which stacks a dozen drinks in a tall, narrow box with a built-in can dispenser.

One Alcoa customer—Coca-Cola Co.—called Fridge Pack the greatest innovation in packaging since Coke's contoured plastic bottle.

ethnography: *n.* the observation and study of people in their natural environments.

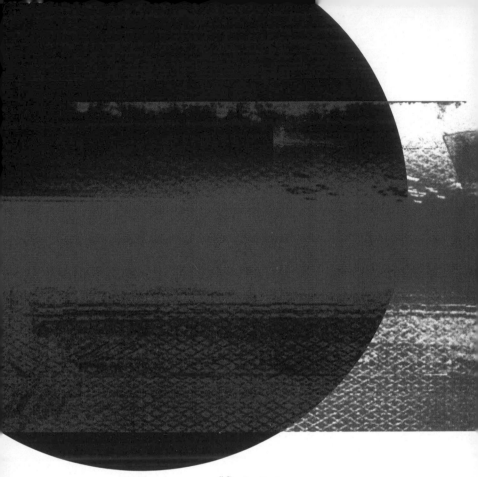

"Curiosity is one
of the most
permanent and
certain characteristics
of a vigorous mind."

—Samuel Johnson

WATCH. ASK. MAYBE EVEN
EAVESDROP.

Procter and Gamble explorers visited customers' homes to check out house-cleaning habits. People told them bathroom cleaning was about as much fun as sticking their hands in wasps' nests. They hated the filthy mess and were frustrated with scrubbing tools not reaching nooks and crannies.

P&G went to work. Designers created MagicReach, a cleaning tool with an adjustable pole, pivoting handle and disposable pads. The pole extends to reach top corners in showers. The handle turns to clean behind toilets. Users never touch dirty pads.

Like P&G, more and more creative firms lock their sensors on customers to detect hot ideas.

When IDEO, the legendary product development firm, designed the interior of Amtrak's express train, its team didn't study the train itself. Instead, explorers focused on the experience of riding the train, watching and talking with more than twenty thousand travelers and employees.

And BuzzMetrics, a leader in word-of-mouth research, explores the Internet—eavesdropping on hundreds of blogs, chat rooms and message boards—to find out what's being said about its clients and coming trends.

ARE YOU EXPLORING BEHIND THE SCENES?

2

EXPLORE

RANGES
OF POSSIBILITY.

exploring on the
FREE RANGE AND FIRING RANGE.

CREATIVE EXPLORING HAPPENS ON TWO LEVELS.

Free-Range exploring is a way of living. A code of curiosity. A 24/7, what's-around-the-corner, check-it-out life skill.

Firing-Range exploring is project specific. A launching pad. The here's-the-job, there's-the-deadline, ready-aim-fire exploring for a specific challenge.

The two types of exploring aren't mutually exclusive. Nor are they either-or propositions. It's difficult to tell where one drops off and the other picks up.

FREE-RANGE EXPLORING OFTEN FLOWS INTO FIRING-RANGE.

And Free-Range exploring gives head starts on deadlines because you're able to pull from insights gathered over time.

FREE-RANGE EXPLORATION

FIRING-RANGE EXPLORATION

YOUR PIERIAN SPRING OF INSIGHTS

pierian spring: *n.* A source of inspiration. (From Greek mythology; a spring in Macedonia, sacred to the Muses.)

"All designers at *Martha Stewart* tend to be collectors, whether it's old books or old type or china patterns or whatever. We go to these pools of resources when we need inspiration for specific projects."

—Kristy Moore,
ART DIRECTOR,
Martha Stewart Living

make FREQUENT DEPOSITS.

Free-Range exploring builds an inspirational bank account to spend when facing deadline-intense projects.

ASK YOURSELF THIS QUESTION:

Am I filling my life with work,
or am I filling my work with life?

FILL YOUR WORK

with life.

FREE-RANGE EXPLORING IS ABOUT FILLING YOUR WORK—AND YOUR-SELF—WITH LIFE.

Leonardo da Vinci was a world-class Free Ranger. Work and life were seamless. He spent his sixty-seven years passionately spotting ideas in nature and elsewhere, then eagerly applying the insights to his work as engineer and artist.

Another great Free-Range explorer was Walt Disney. He harvested ideas from nature, films and, of course, kids. Watching wistful Charlie Chaplin films, Disney conceived Mickey Mouse. Spotting bored children at a run-down play-ground, he imagined Disneyland.

And there's Woody Norris, prolific inventor of devices like HyperSonic Sound, a system that directs sound much like a laser beam directs light. Norris is a Free Ranger, exploring everything from physics to philosophy to religion. He starts broad, he says, going deep when he runs across a topic of interest.

"We encourage Starbucks designers to get a life. Working day and night on your 'work job' doesn't foster inspiration from outside sources."

—Doug Keyes,
SENIOR DESIGNER,
Starbucks

EXPAND YOUR
FREE-RANGE territory.

Maybe you're already living a Free-Range life. Constantly trying new things. Talking to different people. Listening. Watching. Sketching. Writing.

Maybe you Free Range one day and get fenced in the next. Or maybe your curiosity has been forever penned in some not-so-OK corral.

Whatever your status, there's room for more creative roaming.

IT'S A BIG WORLD.

On the next page are four—out of many—categories for Free-Range exploring. Add activities or people in each category. Make these part of your life. Expand your Free Range habits.

ENTERTAINMENT
(MOVIES, THEATER, MUSIC, ZOOS, THEME PARKS, ETC.)

1.

2.

MEDIA
(NEWSPAPERS, MAGAZINES, BOOKS, TV, RADIO, ETC.)

1.

2.

FOOD
(RESTAURANTS, SNACKS, HOME-COOKED MEALS, ETC.)

1.

2.

PEOPLE
(FRIENDS, STRANGERS, CUSTOMERS, COWORKERS, ETC.)

1.

2.

to find solutions,
FIRST GET LOST.

START PROJECTS BY LOSING YOURSELF IN EXPERIENCES.

That's Firing-Range exploration.

Before John Vanderslice grabbed the reins of Club Med, he took an anonymous trip to the club's Cancun property. There he immersed himself in a week-long job on the water ski dock.

Only the property's manager knew that the guy stacking skis and helping guests out of the water would soon be Club Med's CEO. Vanderslice's undercover work helped him spot ideas to serve him well as top executive.

STRONG IDEAS BEGIN WITH FIRING-RANGE EXPLORATION.

Look at iPod. Its creation didn't ignite from stacks of MBA statistics. The starting point, according to Steve Jobs, was to first understand the customer's listening experiences. That kicked off intense Firing-Range exploration into music habits of users.

LOSE YOURSELF IN CUSTOMERS' EXPERIENCES.

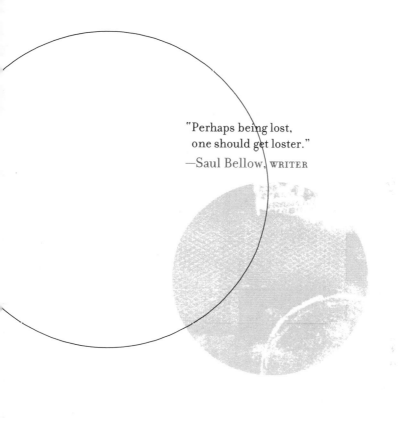

"Perhaps being lost,
one should get loster."
—Saul Bellow, WRITER

360-DEGREE *exploring*

PRINT MEDIA
- books
- magazines
- newspapers
- photos

ENTERTAINMENT
- films
- TV
- music

PERSONAL SURROUNDINGS
- home
- office
- auto

PEERS

FOOD
- restaurants
- snacks
- home cooking
- grocery stores

SCIENCE & BIOLOGY

HARD DATA
- demographics
- surveys
- white papers
- fact sheets

FRIENDS

you

KIDS

OTHER INDUSTRIES

IDEA MASTERS

STRANGERS

CUSTOMERS / CLIENTS

INTERNET

MISTAKES

RETAILERS
- stores
- malls
- displays
- windows

VENUES
- theme parks
- zoos
- museums
- galleries
- clubs

HISTORY
- books
- exhibits

TRANSPORTATION
- airports
- train stations

NATURE
- parks
- mountains
- beaches
- animals
- forests

COMPETITORS

HOW WIDE IS
YOUR WORLD?

1

Where do you get core news about what's happening in the world?

2

How do you keep current on what's happening in your field of work?

3

How do you stay mindful of what's going on in the business world?

4

How do you learn about the interests, needs and lifestyles of age groups older and younger than you?

5

How do you gain insights about the perspectives of the opposite gender?

6

How do you stay current on developments in science and technology?

7

How do you stay aware of trends in entertainment and style—for various age groups and both genders?

8

How do you keep expanding your knowledge of the arts and humanities?

9

How do you become increasingly enlightened about physical, mental, emotional and spiritual well-being?

"Add preparation to command and GOOD THINGS HAPPEN."

—Curt Schilling, BASEBALL PITCHER

Boston Red Sox ace Curt Schilling was always a good pitcher. But he became great when he began exploring before pitching.

Schilling's laptop holds video clips of opposing hitters. Thick notebooks are packed with observations from the dugout. Hundreds of charts tell him how each batter gets hits off him.

Tiger Woods is a similar explorer. In the 2001 U.S. Open, Woods didn't even make the top ten. But he set a goal to win the next year. Months before the 2002 event, he visited its site in Bethpage, New York.

No entourage. No caddy. No cameras. Just Tiger Woods, slowly and quietly walking the course. When he had seen enough, Woods flew home. For weeks, he worked to overcome challenges spotted during his exploration. And he went on to win the U.S. Open.

"Chance favors the prepared mind."
—Louis Pasteur, CHEMIST

WHAT TRAITS
make an IdeaSpotter?

TOLERANT

INDEPENDENT

Witty

CURIOUS

PERSISTENT

OBSERVANT

Questioning

OPTIMISTIC

ENERGETIC

passionate

FLEXIBLE

INTUITIVE

PERCEPTIVE

WHICH TRAITS DO YOU EXHIBIT? WHICH DO YOU NEED TO WORK ON?

"Sometime during the two-year curriculum, every MBA student ought to hear it clearly stated that numbers, techniques and analysis are all side matters. What is central to business is the joy of creating."

—Peter Robinson,
Snapshots from Hell:
The Making of an MBA

3

what you see
IS WHAT YOU GET.

THE MORE you look,
THE MORE YOU find.

In the early 1900s, grocer Walter Deubner watched customers shop his shelves. He noticed purchases were limited to what people could carry in their hands and tuck under their arms.

Deubner spotted an idea. He rigged up a large paper bag reinforced with a cord running through it. The patented Dueubner Shopping Bag held seventy-five pounds, and the cord doubled as a handle.

Deubner was soon selling a million bags a year.

People don't always tell us what they want or need.

Henry Ford said, "If we had asked the public what they wanted, they would have said faster horses."

WATCH PEOPLE IN MOTION.
WHAT DO THEY REALLY NEED?

sweet SOLUTION.

After seeing customers struggle to heat tall bottles of syrup for pancakes, Hungry Jack syrup marketers introduced a short, microwave-ready bottle with a stay-cool handle.

See the
right people.

Hasbro created a new video game. What would cool kids—those vital early adopters—think of it?

To find out, Hasbro explorers visited Chicago playgrounds, skate parks and video arcades looking for what they called Alpha Pups. They asked boys between eight and thirteen: "Who's the coolest kid you know?"

When they got a name, they found that kid and asked the same question.

They kept climbing the cool-kid ladder until they found boys who answered: "Me." They rounded up those coolest kids—the Alpha Pups—handed out prototypes and watched them play the new game.

SEARCH OUT THE RIGHT PEOPLE FOR SMARTER INSIGHTS.

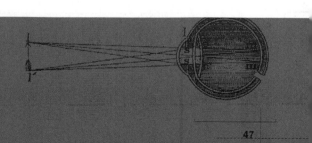

how IDEASPOTTING

STOPPED A CLOSE SHAVE WITH BANKRUPTCY.

In the 1920s, the Odell family's shaving cream firm was heading down the drain. Bankruptcy was only days away.

That's when Allan Odell noticed a series of roadside signs advertising a gas station. If it works for gas, thought Odell, maybe it'll work for shaving cream.

With scrap lumber Odell created the first Burma-Shave signs and staked them along Minnesota's highways, using progressive jingles like:

WITHIN THIS VALE

OF TOIL & SIN

YOUR HEAD GOES BALD

BUT NOT YOUR CHIN

People noticed Odell's signs. They smiled. They told their friends. And Burma-Shave sales jumped to over three million dollars.

The business survived. The signs became advertising icons. All because one guy spotted an idea.

WHAT ARE YOUR EYES SHOWING YOU?

watch THE ROAD.

During the next week, pay extra attention to billboards and other roadside signs. Spot an idea for one of your creative challenges.

"Once in a while
you get shown the light,
In the strangest of places
if you look at it right."
—The Grateful Dead

HOW THE COMICS
KEEP CURRENT.

Do you keep an eye on headlines, fashions and other frames of reference?

Cartoonists do. That's how they make comic strips relevant.

Family Circus kids talk about Google. Blondie uses a laptop. Cookie dresses like a teen pop star. Dick Tracy nails corporate crooks. Little Orphan Annie takes on terrorists.

FIVE CULTURAL REFERENCES
WATCHED BY CARTOONISTS:

· DAILY HEADLINES
· FASHION INDUSTRY
· TV AND MOVIES
· TOY INDUSTRY
· HOME FURNISHINGS INDUSTRY

ARE YOU MONITORING THESE SOURCES FOR INSPIRATION?

headlines
REVEAL BIG MARKETS.

As headlines scream about America's obesity problem, IdeaSpotters take notice. Creative marketers help heavy people either drop pounds or feel more comfortable with their weight. Fast-food chains prepare lighter menus. Health clubs offer weight-loss programs. Apparel firms add plus-size designer clothes. Furniture companies roll out oversize chairs.

ideas sprout in the
STRANGEST OF PLACES.

The U.S. Department of Agriculture released new diet requirements. Not exactly tasty fodder for ideas, right?

WRONG.

When the USDA's report called for more fruits and vegetables, creative food marketers started cooking up ideas.

Sunkist developed Fun Fruit, small packages of fresh fruit for lunch boxes. Grimmway Farms packed petite carrots in microwavable bags. Ready Pac developed packs of apples with peanut butter dip. And a food trade group convinced supermarkets to add refrigerated cases with cut fruits and vegetables at checkout.

What new developments are happening in your world? Scan news releases, white papers, even dull reports.

YOUR NEXT IDEA MAY BE GROWING BETWEEN THE LINES.

eat that WRAPPER.

To make fruits and vegetables more convenient, the USDA helped develop vegetable- and fruit-based edible film. For example, fresh-cut apple pieces are wrapped in film made of apple puree to maintain freshness and reduce browning.

IDEAS LIVE IN
lifestyles.

FURNITURE COMPANIES ARE PROS AT MONITORING LIFESTYLES.

For example, when sales of second homes spiked in America, furniture firms paid attention.

For beach homes, Stanley Furniture created mahogany pieces resembling furniture from Caribbean islands. Basset downsized bedroom pieces to easily fit into smaller second homes.

America's poker craze also inspired furniture designs. Hooker Furniture, for example, created card tables with reversible tops to convert into dining tables.

Noticing its customers' growing fascination with reclaimed objects, Seely furniture created beds out of wood from old factories. And Staples Cabinet Makers' kitchen islands are made of beams from old barns.

WHAT CAN YOU CREATE FOR SHIFTING INTERESTS?

Look into *lifestyles.*

WHAT PUBLICATIONS, WEB SITES AND
EVENTS CAN HELP YOU MONITOR THE
LIFESTYLES OF YOUR AUDIENCES?

	PUBLICATIONS	WEB SITES	EVENTS
FASHION			
FOOD			
MUSIC			
SPORTS			
HOMES			
HOBBIES			
OUTDOORS			
POLITICS			
OTHERS			

HOW TO *notice*
DETAILS.

IdeaSpotting depends on details. Here's one way to polish your noticing skills.

Think about a street you often walk or drive down. List everything you remember about that street. You'll soon realize there's much you can't recall—the color of a building, the name of the dry-cleaners, the number of parking spaces.

The next day spend a few extra minutes on the street. Notice every detail. Write down what you see. Make a precise map.

Wait a few days, then give yourself another test. If you've forgotten anything, return to the street and correct mistakes.

Do this exercise with magazine pages, retail shops and office spaces.

Each time you're reminding your brain that details count. And you're training yourself to retrieve details from memory.

rashomon effect: *n.*
The effect of the subjectivity of perception. For every event there are X versions of what happened, with X equal to or greater than the number of witnesses. A well-known phenomenon to detectives, reporters and creative explorers!

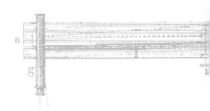

HOW TO speed-read
A ROOM.

A supermarket has more than 30,000 products. A video store has 5,000 titles. People are packed in subways, restaurants and malls.

You can't see it all. So what's the answer?

Scan and select. Train yourself to speed-read details, braking for what's inspiring. Teach your brain to point and shoot.

Here's your assignment: When you enter a space, quickly scan and record first impressions. How does the space feel? What's the mood? What colors and characteristics jump out? What's the smell? What sounds do you hear?

Then take mental snapshots of key areas and interesting people. Etch each image into your memory. Close your eyes. See the picture. Catalog details.

TRAIN YOUR SUBCONSCIOUS TO FILTER SUPERFLUOUS AND CAPTURE SIGNIFICANT.

GET A SQUIRREL'S camera.

Ever wonder how squirrels find all those nuts they hide? They make mental snapshots, according to Dr. Temple Grandin, an autistic person who uses her autism to help explore animal behavior. After burying a nut, the squirrel looks right and left before moving on. He's taking mental pictures of physical coordinates, reports Dr. Grandin, and the visual memory later helps him recover the nut.

SEE WHERE YOU'RE
STANDING.

SEEING ISN'T JUST LOOKING. IT'S ALSO POSITIONING FOR PRIME VIEWS.

That may mean elbowing in. Or stepping back. Or going high above, left or right.

Try this: Visit a gallery and stand six feet from a painting. Record your impressions. Take a few steps left or right. Note changes in your reactions. Now come within inches of the artwork. See and feel what happens.

This basic exercise proves a point. If you have difficulty finding ideas, maybe you're in the wrong spot.

Perhaps move closer, engaging one-on-one.

"Lots of companies look at customers as if they're zoo exhibitions," says Mark Rodgers, Pearlfisher's insight director. "We believe in close contact."

Or maybe step back and look at cultural factors.

"I'm always observing how different cultures use public spaces," says Tony Reich, an environmental-space architect. "People in Saudi Arabia have different personal-space boundaries than people in Shanghai. I stand back and look at how people interact."

KNOW WHERE YOU STAND. YOU MAY BE SHOULDER-TO-SHOULDER WITH A GREAT IDEA.

LIKING BROCCOLI
isn't the same as eating it.

A boy goes to dinner at a friend's house, and the mother asks if he likes broccoli.

"Sure," says the boy. "I like broccoli fine."

During dinner, however, the mother sees the boy hasn't touched the broccoli.

"I thought you said you liked broccoli," says the mother.

"Oh, I like it," replies the boy. "I just don't eat it."

WATCH WHAT PEOPLE DO
RATHER THAN JUST ASK FOR THEIR
OPINIONS. WHAT THEY TELL YOU
OFTEN BELIES THEIR BEHAVIOR.

"We look at real rather than reported behavior."

—Mark Rodgers,
INSIGHT DIRECTOR,
Pearlfisher

LOOK HOW THAT
PERSON *behaves.*

CONSUMERS OFTEN SAY ONE THING, THEN DO SOMETHING ELSE.

That's because buying tends to be an emotional and instinctual process. Consumers buy on emotion, then rationalize the decision with reasoning.

More than ninety percent of decision making actually happens in the subconscious, believes Harvard professor Gerald Zaltman, building a strong case for observing consumers on emotional levels.

Yet for years marketers and advertisers have used the AIDA research model: Attention, Interest, Desire, Action.

Many forward-thinking researchers—including the Advertising Research Foundation—believe AIDA methods stop short because they discount emotional elements.

"You often can't get to insights and ideas through purely quantitative and qualitative research," says Monica Little of Little and Company. "It takes talking with people, watching people, seeing how people really make decisions."

ARE YOU WATCHING?

"There are two reasons for doing anything. A good reason and the real reason."

—J.P. Morgan

black-hole EXPLORING

Sometimes you can determine traits about your audiences only as astronomers discern black holes—from their effects on things around them.

Your brain
IS A HOUSE OF MIRRORS.

Mirror neurons are another good reason to watch people.

As we observe others, mirroring brain cells recreate their experiences within us.

Seeing a guy smack his thumb with a hammer activates the neurons in your brain that fire if you whack your own thumb. Likewise, if you watch a person being touched, neurons that process touch will also fire in you.

Neuroscientists say mirror neurons connect to the limbic system, the brain's emotional center. When mirror neurons fire, they trigger empathic emotions.

Because of mirror neurons, you don't simply see what other people are doing as you watch them. You're actually feeling sensations in your own brain as if you were doing these actions.

By closely watching your audience, you begin to experience their experience.

This leads to understanding. And understanding leads to inspiration.

Watch people interact in restaurants, parks, airports.

Let mirror neurons fire away. Record your experience.

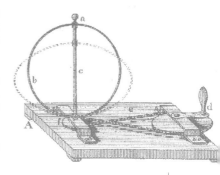

FACE facts.

A husband's raised eyebrow says he's doubtful. A friend's crooked smile says she's kidding. A mother's wrinkled brow says she's worried.

And that only scratches the flesh of face-to-face awareness.

Two psychologists, Paul Ekman and Wallace Friesen, pegged three thousand facial configurations signaling thoughts and emotions. They even put together a Facial Action Coding System (FACS) for reading expressions.

FACS helps medical researchers study everything from heart disease to schizophrenia. And Pixar and DreamWorks designers consulted FACS to animate characters in *Toy Story* and *Shrek*.

You may not want to master FACS, but its efficacy shows observation's value.

ARE YOU PAYING ATTENTION TO FACIAL EXPRESSIONS, BODY LANGUAGE AND OTHER VISUAL SIGNALS OF YOUR AUDIENCES?

casting ballots
FOR FACES.

Princeton researchers asked volunteers to pick the most competent political candidate after glimpsing picture pairs for one second. Candidates that volunteers deemed most competent—just from a glance—actually won in most Senate and House elections.

HAVE FACE time.

PRACTICE CATCHING VISUAL CUES.
OBSERVE THREE PEOPLE TOMORROW.

PERSON:

1. *male teen at airport*
2.
3.

EXPRESSION OR BODY LANGUAGE:

1. *sneer*
2.
3.

SIGNAL:

1. *cockiness*
2.
3.

WANT/NEED:

1. *girl's attention!*
2.
3.

read CLUES.

Autistic people are often thought to have mind-reading abilities. But according to Dr. Temple Grandin, autistic herself, that's not the case. Autistic individuals are students of minute details, she points out, and they sometimes detect another person's pattern of behavior by subconsciously assembling these details.

"We all give clues about what we're doing or what we're getting ready to do," says Dr. Grandin. "The autistic individual is simply reading these clues."

"An observant person sees things overlooked by others... A really good scientist—or a really good artist for that matter, anyone whose mind and soul are capable of some extension—sees what is going on, sees the patterns, and asks, 'Why?'

"What underlying forces are at work? How are those forces exerting themselves? How may we understand?..."

—Carl Safina, *Song for the Blue Ocean*

GET A PICTURE OF *that.*

IDEO WAS ASKED TO REDESIGN A HOSPITAL'S
WAITING ROOMS.

The team began by having hospital staffers bring
in photos of their families enjoying memorable
moments. Most snapshots showed families in
circular configurations—around dinner tables,
around Christmas trees, around campfires.

These shots underscored the need for round
tables in waiting rooms, explained IDEO, where
families could eat and talk.

Instead of photos, Reich + Petch architects use
Post-it notes. In early client meetings, they'll distribute pads and ask everyone to write one word
capturing their vision for the project.

"What surprises participants is how the words
tend to be visceral rather than academic," says
Tony Reich. "This reminds them—and us—that the
true vision is to create an emotional experience
for the end user."

photo EVIDENCE.

Ask clients or end users to bring in snapshots conveying their feelings about a particular project. Or have each person write a word that captures the project's essence. Post photos or words on a wall. Collectively discuss their significance in terms of end-user experiences.

YOU see more
THAN YOU THINK.

An old man witnessed a traffic accident, and in court the defense attorney tried to discredit his testimony.

"Mr. Bristow, I see you wear thick glasses," said the lawyer.

"Yes, sir, I do."

"And you're up in age, aren't you?"

"Yes, sir—eighty-four in May."

"So exactly how far can you see, Mr. Bristow?"

The old guy thought for a minute. "Well, sir, I can see the moon. How far is that?"

DON'T UNDERESTIMATE OBSERVATION'S REACH.

4

LISTENING 101:

a. CLOSE MOUTH.

b. OPEN EARS.

WHEN YOU LISTEN,
you spot IDEAS.

Pattye Moore, Sonic's former president, listened as customers talked about the fast-food chain's menu. One woman wondered out loud why Sonic couldn't wrap a pancake around link sausage.

Moore spotted an idea. Her test kitchen went to work, and Pancake on a Stick soon became Sonic's hottest-selling breakfast item.

Nestle wanted to sell more bottled water in Italy, especially to youngsters.

So company explorers started listening. Italian mothers told them loud and clear that they believed fizzy drinks were not good for their children. Nestle spotted an idea and created Issima, a brand of still water just for kids.

Exploring for a Sprite campaign, Ogilvy's Brand Integration Group listened to one young consumer say Sprite felt "like a chill explosion of lemon-lime icicles going down my throat."

Ogilvy's team spotted an idea. The comment inspired visually exploding designs that morph from cans to basketball goals to giant murals.

ACTIVE LISTENING CALLS FOR FOCUSING ON WHAT'S SAID, CARING ABOUT THE PERSON SAYING IT, AND HUSTLING TO USE WHAT YOU'VE HEARD.

"An artist has to keep one ear to the ground and one to the heart."

—Bruce Springsteen

HOW TO LISTEN IF
YOU LIKE TO TALK.
Or if you don't.

If you're outgoing, you may define listening as the gap before you talk again.

Instead, practice truly listening while the other person talks. Focus on her words. Don't jump in after every sentence. Think before opening your mouth.

On the other hand, if you're reserved, you may spend listening time fretting over how to respond.

Relax. Just listen. When you have something to say, say it. Otherwise, let body language and verbal reactions show the person you're listening.

"There are two types of people in the world. Those who come in the room and say, 'Well, here I am!' and those who come into a room and say, 'Ah, there you are.'"

—Frederick L. Collins,
WRITER

THE POLITICS OF
listening.

Political views aside, you'll probably agree that Bill and Hillary Clinton are both cogent communicators.

Their secret is listening to constituents, then responding to what they hear.

Bill Clinton won crucial town-hall debates in his first presidential campaign by leaving the podium, moving toward his audience and carefully listening as citizens asked questions. He then responded directly to questioners.

Many New Yorkers considered Hillary Clinton an outsider when she first ran for the Senate. To overcome those criticisms, she organized listening tours, traveling across the state to learn the needs and opinions of voters.

Political tactics? Absolutely. But the Clintons' listening skills gave them insights and ideas to create winning campaigns.

"Most people will not really listen or pay attention to your point of view until they become convinced you have heard and appreciate theirs."

—Ralph Nichols,
SALES TRAINER

LISTEN UP.

EMBARK ON YOUR OWN
LISTENING TOUR WITH:

- END USERS
- CLIENTS
- SUPPLIERS
- EMPLOYEES
- TEAM MEMBERS
- OPINION SHAPERS

WHAT'S YOUR
listening level?

WE USUALLY LISTEN AT ONE OF FOUR LEVELS:

- · WE IGNORE THE PERSON
- · WE PRETEND TO LISTEN
- · WE SELECTIVELY LISTEN
- · WE ATTENTIVELY LISTEN

A fifth and more effective level is empathic listening, according to experts like Stephen Covey. At that level, you strive to fully understand the person's words and feelings.

You listen with ears and eyes—and with your heart.

Empathic listeners seek first to understand before trying to be understood. That means putting aside your own views and getting inside the other person's thoughts and words.

PRACTICE EMPATHIC LISTENING WITH TWO PEOPLE TODAY.

"I would say that listening to the other person's emotions may be the most important thing I've learned in twenty years of business."

—Heath Herber,
FOUNDER,
Herber Company

BUILD YOUR
ear muscles.

EXERCISE #1
Sit outside and close your eyes. Take a few breaths and relax. Listen to what's happening around you—birds singing, people talking, wind blowing, whatever. Identify each sound.

EXERCISE #2
Stretch your hearing. While still sitting outside, act as if you have supernatural hearing that's like a directional mike. Turn your head and focus one ear in a specific direction. Listen for a faint sound in the distance. Bring it closer. Mentally pull the sound toward you.

EXERCISE #3
Cup your right hand behind your right ear and cup your left hand in front of your left ear. Notice how you can hear noises from behind with your left ear and noises in front with your right ear. Reverse the process and listen again. Pay attention to how this affects hearing and perception.

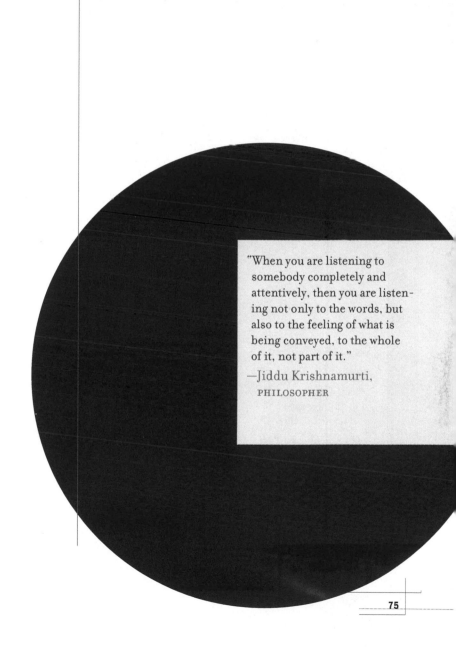

"When you are listening to somebody completely and attentively, then you are listening not only to the words, but also to the feeling of what is being conveyed, to the whole of it, not part of it."

—Jiddu Krishnamurti,
PHILOSOPHER

SEVEN DEADLY SINS
of BAD LISTENERS.

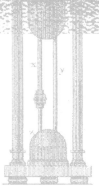

1. PREJUDGING WHAT THE SPEAKER IS ABOUT TO SAY.

2. SILENTLY BASHING DELIVERY OR APPEARANCE.

3. THINKING ABOUT WHAT TO SAY NEXT.

4. INTERRUPTING THE SPEAKER.

5. GIVING IN TO DISTRACTIONS.

6. FINISHING THE SPEAKER'S THOUGHTS.

7. TUNING OUT.

WHAT'S YOUR LISTENING SIN?
REPENT.

"Listening is a magnetic and strange thing, a creative force…"

—Dr. Karl Menninger, PSYCHIATRIST

LISTEN WITHOUT
multitasking.

WHEN ON THE PHONE, WHAT ELSE ARE YOU UP TO?

Shuffling through paperwork? Checking e-mail? Going through your wallet? Trying to catch the eye of that hottie in the hall?

Studies show over 75 percent of people admit to doing other activities while on the phone.

That's fine if the voice on the other end belongs to a solicitor or bureaucrat. But if it's somebody you should listen to, put aside other stuff.

EARS CAN'T SPOT IDEAS WHILE EYES SPOT DISTRACTIONS.

Write the word "Listen!" on a Post-it.

Stick It on your phone.

"It takes two to speak the truth—one to speak and another to hear."

—Henry David Thoreau

HAVE *big ears.*

Early jazz players praised a fellow musician by saying he or she had "big ears"—meaning the person actively listened to another's playing and built on rhythm, lyrics and tempo.

HAVE BIG EARS WHEN YOU'RE TALKING WITH OTHERS—WHETHER WITH ONE PERSON, TWO PEOPLE OR A TEAM. SPOT IDEAS AND BUILD ON THEM.

you don't know
WHAT YOU'VE GOT UNTIL YOU LOSE IT.

Next Saturday, buy a pair of earplugs. Wear them for a few hours as you go about your day. Record in your notebook how it feels to have restricted hearing abilities. Remove earplugs. Review what you've written. Be grateful. Listen.

heard any
GOOD STORIES LATELY?

STORIES HAVE FOREVER BEEN CULTURAL THREADS. THEY HELP MAKE SENSE OF OUR WORLD.

And IdeaSpotters embrace stories to help them better understand audiences.

Listen as people tell stories about themselves. One tells a tale filled with conflict and struggle. Another presents a quest for excitement. Another offers a narrative of hope.

Stoke stories. Ask people to describe a workday or weekend. Inquire about families. Find out about dreams. Beg for examples.

As head of Xerox, Anne Mulcahy urges employees to tell her stories about their work. "Everyone has a story," she says, "whether it's saving a buck or doing something different for customers."

LISTEN AS PEOPLE SPILL STORIES. YOU'LL HEAR DRAMATIC IDEAS.

"'Tell me a story' still comprise four of the most powerful words in English."

—Pat Conroy, AUTHOR

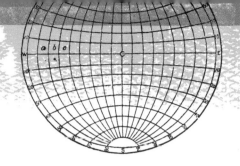

HOW LISTENING SPARKED
THE WORLD'S BEST JINGLE.

McDonald's "You deserve a break today" ranks as the best jingle of all time, according to *Advertising Age*.

THAT'S BECAUSE SOMEBODY LISTENED.

"We spent hours and hours listening to women who were still called housewives back in 1971," says Keith Reinhard of DDB Worldwide.

They heard all about the women's daily routines— how they planned meals, ran out of menu ideas, wanted to please their families.

Reinhard then created a jingle that played back what the customers were saying.

NOW THERE'S A GAME PLAN FOR CREATIVE SUCCESS:

1. listen to what your audience tells you
2. learn about their hopes, fears, dreams
3. play back experiences as story, song, image

YOU'LL PROBABLY WIN AWARDS. YOU'LL DEFINITELY WIN HEARTS.

"I have no aesthetic beyond telling a really incredible story that people are moved by."

—Brian Collins,
BRAND INTEGRATION GROUP,
Ogilvy & Mather

5

ASK THE QUESTION, PLAY THE FOOL.

DON'T ASK
THE QUESTION,

STAY THE FOOL.

NOTICE HOW
creative people
ARE THE ONES ASKING QUESTIONS?

Lots of people saw apples fall. Sir Isaac Newton asked why and explained gravity.

Lots of people wanted instant photos. Edwin Land asked how and invented Polaroid cameras.

Lots of people wanted fast shipping. Fred Smith asked when and started FedEx.

Lots of people wanted a monument to honor Americans killed in Vietnam. Maya Lin asked where and created a gripping memorial.

Questions determine fate—whether we'll explore or stagnate, create or vegetate.

What's on your mind today?
Write down six questions about it.

Ask, ask, ask, ask, ask, ask.

"The important thing is not to stop questioning."

—Albert Einstein

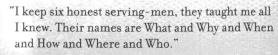

"I keep six honest serving-men, they taught me all I knew. Their names are What and Why and When and How and Where and Who."

—Rudyard Kipling

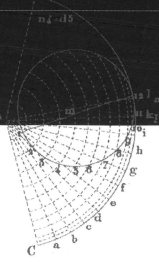

QUIT ASKING
the same *tired questions.*

Michael Dell, founder of Dell Computers, likes asking different questions. If he can't think of a different question, he asks the same question in a different way.

"I have no special talents. I am only passionately curious."

—Albert Einstein

Original questions help Dell get insights about his firm, market and users.

"A major stimulant to creative thinking is focused questions," says marketing advisor Brian Tracy. "A well-worded question penetrates to the heart of the matter and triggers new ideas."

Monica Little, principal of Little & Company, agrees. "We never simply ask end users if they like this or that," she says. "We focus questions on a visceral level—'how does this make you feel?' or 'what does this remind you of?'"

Right now something in your world needs a new approach.

ONE CLEAR, PENETRATING QUESTION MIGHT MAKE ALL THE DIFFERENCE.

What's the question?

HOW *one* QUESTION

PUT MEAT ON BARE BONES.

Reich + Petch, an experience architecture firm, often designs natural history museums, including the Smithsonian's Hall of Mammals.

"Exploring the design for one museum, we asked the curator to show us something that really interested her," says Steven Petri, exhibits director. "She pointed to a few bones that, quite frankly, looked like garbage to uneducated eyes."

But the curator explained that bones were historical evidence.

"She talked passionately about how bones let scientists know what the animal looked like, what it ate, how it died," says Petri. "Listening to her, we got ideas on how to exhibit the artifacts."

Reich + Petch relies on questions for fast insights.

"We can't tell the client we'll be back in a year after we've totally researched the project," says Tony Reich, a founding principal. "We have to move rapidly toward ideas— and our best technique is asking lots of questions."

WHEN IS YOUR NEXT CLIENT MEETING?
LIST SIX CREATIVE QUESTIONS YOU'LL ASK:

1.   ?
2.   ?
3.   ?
4.   ?
5.   ?
6.   ?

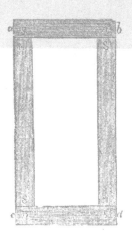

KIDS ASK

BETTER QUESTIONS *than adults.*

Children don't pull punches. They aren't afraid of looking dumb
or silly. And they don't try to impress with the caliber of their
questions.

Little kids ask things like:

- HOW COME THE SKY IS BLUE?
- HOW COME DOGS HAVE COLD NOSES?
- HOW COME CHICKENS DON'T FLY LIKE DUCKS?
- HOW COME WE DON'T HAVE DESSERT AFTER BREAKFAST?
- HOW COME DAD DOESN'T SHAVE HIS LEGS LIKE MOM?

Not getting answers you need?

TURN LOFTY QUESTIONS INTO
"HOW COME" QUESTIONS.

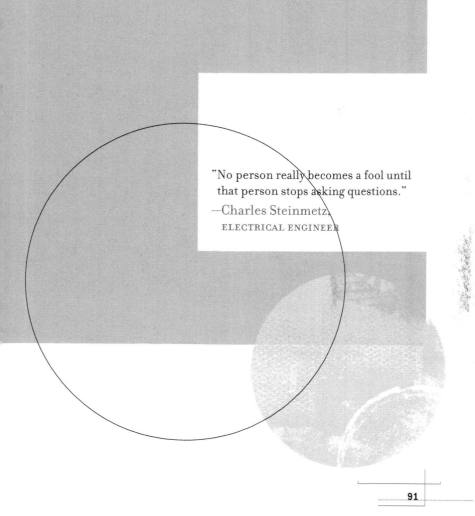

"No person really becomes a fool until
that person stops asking questions."
—Charles Steinmetz,
ELECTRICAL ENGINEER

6

KNOW WHAT
MAKES YOUR AUDIENCE

LAUGH, CRY AND SCREAM.

KNOW WHAT CUSTOMERS DO
ON SATURDAY NIGHT.

Eva Maddox, design principal of Perkins + Will, is a pioneer in the world of branded environments. And she gets to know her audiences.

"We engage people at all levels—officers to janitors," she says. "We want to find out not only what they do for work, but what they do for fun."

Designing the Oak Park Public Library, Maddox held town-hall meetings to find out what Oak Park residents really expected from their library.

"Sure, it would be quicker to just go in a room and come up with something," she says, "but that usually results in faulty answers."

Cultural immersion also helped Maddox design a children's hospital in New Mexico.

"About twenty Native American tribes are part of the community," she said. "We invited spokespersons from all tribes and sat around discussing

likes and dislikes. Those engagements helped us discover insights and avoid pitfalls."

Maddox is also a founder of Archeworks, an alternative design school that creates solutions for nonprofits. One project involved products to assist victims of Alzheimer's.

After getting to know caregivers, Archeworks students designed a walker that also helps patients slide in and out of cars. This benefits caregivers as well as patients.

"Our real customers are often our customers' customers," says Maddox.

you're
NOT THE CUSTOMER.

That's one of two signs posted at Dell. (The other is: Listen to the customer.)

At Dell's usability lab, explorers watch customers use products.

Seeing customers struggle with volume control, they spotted the need for easy accessibility. Dell's Pocket DJ now has a prominent volume-control button.

Whirlpool is another firm that looks to its customers for ideas.

Chuck Jones, head of Whirlpool design, thinks of customers as co-collaborators in the creative process. Seeing users trying to jam six-packs into tight refrigerator shelves, Whirlpool designers created Kenmore Elite's roomy door shelf.

And some companies really get down and dirty with customers. Clorox explorers went into customers' bathrooms and watched them scrub toilets. This latrine duty led to Toilet Wand, a toilet brush with a disposable head.

DO YOU REALLY KNOW YOUR USERS?

"We have a program called Follow Me Home, where we literally follow consumers into their homes and watch them use our products."

—Jacqueline Maartense,
EXECUTIVE VICE PRESIDENT,
Corel

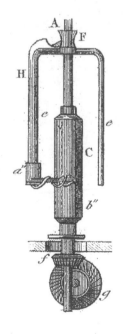

"Directly witnessing and experiencing aspects of behavior in the real world is a proven way of inspiring and informing new ideas."

—Jane Fulton Suri, IDEO

GOING TO BAT
for customers.

As Louisville Slugger's operations director, Chuck Schupp makes sure major leaguers have the bats they want and need.

And he doesn't just read sports pages to learn about his audience.

Throughout the season, Schupp visits one team after another, meeting with batting coaches and players. He finds out about hitters and their bats. What's working. What's not working. What might make things better.

Some players want traditional bats made of white ash. Others prefer maple. Some want flared handles. Others want bigger knobs on the end.

When players complained about ash's flaking and maple's hardness, Schupp had Louisville Slugger seek out other woods. The company is now trying out Norwegian beech bats with major- and minor-league players.

And when hitters told Schupp of their needs for increased bat speed, Louisville Slugger developed lighter bats. The lowest-weight bat used to be 32.5 ounces. The company now makes bats as low as 31 ounces.

ARE YOUR CUSTOMERS IN A SLUMP?

WHAT IDEAS WOULD PULL THEM OUT?

immersion =
UNDERSTANDING.

Michael Lewis, author of *Liar's Poker* and *Moneyball*, immerses by traveling with those he writes about. He believes people are more interesting and revealing when moving rather than sitting still.

Susan Orleans, *New Yorker* staff writer, is another who believes in immersion's power. She embedded herself in Miami days before the Super Bowl and settled into Sydney weeks before the Olympics.

"The way I report is to immerse myself in something I usually know very little about," she writes, "and what I experience is the journey toward a grasp of what I've seen."

Preparing for his Broadway role in *Julius Caesar*, Denzel Washington hired a Shakespearean expert and spent eight hours a day, six days a week,

"understanding Shakespeare's world, understanding the play... and trying to understand what everybody's saying to me."

HOW DEEP ARE YOU DIVING?

listen TO THE BEAT.

Hot Topic, a chain of stores for teens, bases its fashions on music and musicians. Designers and buyers live the lifestyle, immersing themselves in the music world. "Everything About the Music" is Hot Topic's tag line, and its exploring mantra is to always be "street up, not design down."

dive into your business—
and your customer's.

Before becoming Motorola's CEO, Edward Zander immersed himself in the company and its culture.

He read all he could about Motorola and its competitors. He visited with employees and customers. He talked with former Motorola executives. And he interviewed other CEOs about leading a major firm.

Kevin Sharer took a similar dive. Just after becoming CEO at Amgen, Sharer interviewed the company's top 100 executives—despite the fact he had been Amgen's president for the past eight years.

"Whether or not you are new to the company, you have to bring in a new set of eyes," he explained.

watch COMPETITORS.

Daniel Negreanu, TV poker's megastar, looks at tournament footage the way a ball player watches game tapes. He searches for what poker players call "tells"—facial or behavioral clues that an opponent is bluffing or holding a loaded hand.

Review behavioral cues of competitors. What tells do you see?

WHO *tips you off*?

"We don't see things as they are. We see things as we are."
—Anaïs Nin, writer

WHO CAN HELP YOU SEE YOUR ORGANIZATION WITH NEW EYES?

1.

2.

3.

WHO CAN HELP YOU SEE YOUR CLIENT'S ORGANIZATION WITH NEW EYES?

1.

2.

3.

WHO CAN HELP YOU SEE END USERS WITH NEW EYES?

1.

2.

3.

WHO CAN HELP YOU SEE COMPETITORS WITH NEW EYES?

1.

2.

3.

leopard and lizard.

Mental evolution gives us what amounts to three brains in one:
· The lizard—or reptilian—brain of survival instincts
· The leopard brain of emotions (limbic system)
· The intellectual brain of learning and reasoning

Consumers commonly call on the leopard and lizard brains—rather than the intellectual brain—for buying decisions.

The leopard brain gives emotional reasons to buy that iMac or Harley.

And, as Dr. G.C. Rapaille teaches, imprints in the reptilian or lizard brain spur purchases of that PT Cruiser or can of Folgers.

Apple spots great ideas by seeing the leopard and lizard in its cultlike audience.

"The starting point for iPod wasn't a chip or a design," says Steve Jobs. "The starting point was the question, 'What's the user experience?'"

Backbone data seldom provides emotional and instinctual perspectives.

FIND THE LEOPARD AND LIZARD.

"We believe the place to start every project is with a look through the customer's eyes."

—Joe Duffy,
DUFFY & PARTNERS

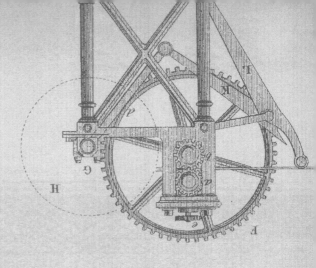

"You can say the right thing about a product and nobody will listen. You've got to say it in such a way that people will feel it in their gut. Because if they don't feel it, nothing will happen."

—Bill Bernbach, ADVERTISING PIONEER

"together WE GET SMART."

Little and Company, a branding firm, practices immersion when exploring for ideas.

"During discovery, we collaborate with everybody," says Monica Little. "Internal teams, client teams and end users all help illuminate the situation. Together we get smart."

"Qualitative and quantitative research are extremely useful—but there's usually a huge gap between logical and linear research and actionable, emotional insights needed to connect with users."

To reach the emotional level, Little plunges into organizations and their operations.

Working on concepts for the Minnesota Historical Society, her team sifted through volumes of qualitative research—then fanned out to engage twenty-four site managers across the state.

"We wanted a firsthand look at the frontline people," says Little. "These are the folks who will live with our ideas."

Her team members mimic private investigators. "We sniff out trails, look for clues, follow intuition," she says. "We use the Columbo method of asking lots of open-ended questions."

ARE YOU AND YOUR AUDIENCE WORKING TOGETHER?

MAKE INSIGHTS
easy to see.

Spotting insights isn't the end of the freeway. We have to proffer insights in a user-friendly form.

"We've had clients point to millions of dollars worth of their traditional research and say, 'It's all interesting, but I don't know what to do with it,'" says Lisa Maulhardt of Stone Yamashita Partners.

Stone Yamashita has built a practice around extracting insights from data and making those insights tangible to clients.

"TO BE WORTHWHILE," SAYS MAULHARDT, "INSIGHTS MUST HELP CLIENTS SOLVE PROBLEMS, FOCUS THEIR TEAMS, AND DETERMINE WHERE TO INVEST TIME AND MONEY."

Decks of "insight cards" are one method used by Stone Yamashita to make its findings obvious, provocative and compelling for clients.

"Holding up a deck of these cards, one company president told us, 'I love being able to carry the fuel for a multimillion-dollar strategy in my shirt pocket,'" says Maulhardt.

ARE YOUR INSIGHTS TO CLIENTS INEXPRESSIVE OR INGENIOUS?

watch
FOR THE
WOW FACTOR

Tony Reich, a Toronto architect, pays attention to how people react to an attraction, be it the Grand Canyon or a grand piano.

"I'm always looking for the wow factor—what thrills people, what makes them stop and take notice," he says. "I want those same reactions in spaces we design."

Tom Otterness also looks for reactions, calling New York streets his laboratory. Otterness creates playful, storybook sculptures, many permanently positioned around the city. He spends hours secretly watching kids and adults react to his sculptures, then takes insights back to the studio, incorporating them into his next pieces.

Richard Tait, co-creator of Cranium, likes to imagine how the wow factor looks as he begins creating games. He calls it "moment engineering"—visualizing the perfect moment customers will experience when playing the game.

For example, before Tait's team began designing a children's game, they drew a picture of a mother sitting around the floor with her kids on a rainy day. She and the children were laughing and high-fiving as they played the game. That image became the team's creative goal.

ARE YOU WATCHING FOR WOWS?

"Antiques often inspire our home collection of products. But we don't want to replicate. We look at an antique and ask ourselves, 'What is it about this piece that has made people cherish it for decades?' We're after the emotional connection and how we can create that for today's consumers."

—Jeff Wilson,
PRESIDENT,
Midwest of Cannon Falls

wow WORKSHEET.

Go where people react to stimuli—a zoo, city street, amusement venue, museum, gallery, mall or other retail space.

Observe first reactions. Notice emotional connections. Do people smile or laugh? Frown or shake their heads? Stay still or move closer? Stand alone or join others? Linger or rush on?

location/object	audience description	reactions

HOW CAN THESE OBSERVATIONS HELP YOU WOW YOUR AUDIENCE?

PICK A PROJECT.

Draw or describe how the wow factor or perfect moment might look as an audience discovers your creation.

Now—make it happen!

7

IF AN IDEA POPS UP,
write it down.

IF A VISION
DRIFTS IN,
SKETCH IT OUT.

capture ideas and *insights.*

WE FIND IDEAS ONE SECOND, FORGET THEM THE NEXT.

That's why it's smart to jot down ideas and insights when they pop up. Book them before they flee.

Leonardo da Vinci is one of history's most famous note takers. His notebooks overflowed with observations on nature, art, and architecture.

Thomas Edison loaded thousands of notebooks with insights and diagrams.

And today's creative people are equally diligent about note taking. Canadian designer Bruce Mau says, "The single most necessary device for me is a notebook... I just plow through notebooks."

Gail Anderson, previously *Rolling Stone* art director and now at SpotCo, calls herself a note taker and language observer. "I love making notes about type I've seen on store signs or sides of buildings," she says.

Note taking gives the creative process time to breath, say Erin Whelan, *Real Simple* art director. "I like recording really out-there ideas," she says, "It's so great to start at crazy places and then reach smart solutions."

Doug Keyes, Starbucks senior designer, agrees: "Kernels of ideas tend to breed bigger ideas."

GRAB IDEAS WHILE THEY LAST. TAKE NOTES.

A FEW NOTES ON
TAKING NOTES.

Capture words. Sketch images. Avoid long sentences and elaborate drawings.

You're after what Henry James called "the floating particle of an idea."

Try tree-branching, which is much like using mindmaps for brainstorming. Write your key word and circle it. Build branches supporting other words, symbols, and ideas.

DEVELOP PERSONAL SHORTHAND. IF IT MAKES SENSE TO YOU, GO FOR IT.

If you want to be more anal, possibly borrow from the Cornell Note Taking System. Divide off the left one-fourth of your page with a vertical line. Use the right side to record thoughts. Use the left side to reduce those thoughts into key words for recall.

RECALL	RECORD

MAN/TRAIN SEAT

old letters/book

"CIRCUS TRICK"

Wednesday's client presentation

note–TAKING TIP

Write a key word in the top right corner of each filled sheet in your notebook. When trying to find info later, you can easily thumb through the pages.

GOING BEYOND GOOGLE.
Here are a few other search tools to try if Google doesn't give you what you need.

A9.COM
This search engine from Amazon.com includes images, media columns and blogs in its first search.

ANSWERS.COM
Includes authoritative sources, such as Merriam Webster and Columbia University Press.

CLUSTY.COM
Clusters the results from other search engines, sorting by category.

GROKKER.COM
Visual people often like this Yahoo-powered engine that shows results with a graph containing circles filled with dots.

HOTBOT.COM AND INFO.COM
Both provide Google results along with those of other search engines.

shorthand WITH GOOGLE'S HELP.
With today's search engines, note taking often becomes easier. Train yourself to record important names and key words. You can later Google these words for specifics.

WRITE IN the right notebook.

Moleskines are the drug of choice for many creative folks. For a couple of centuries, Moleskine (mol-a-skeen'-a) notebooks have been favored by artists, writers and other creative people, including Matisse, Hemingway and Picasso.

Raving fans shout about the Moleskine, a simple black rectangle secured with an elastic band. The paper feels good under the pen, and a small accordion folder in the back is perfect for a few photos, index cards or clippings.

"I love my Moleskines," says Kristy Moore, art director at *Martha Stewart Living*. "I keep two going all the time. One is my inspirational book filled with quotes, clippings and other stimuli. The other is my daily recorder and list keeper."

To learn more about Moleskines and their fans, visit www.moleskineus.com and www.moleskinerie.com.

Miquelrius notebooks, made in Spain, receive accolades not unlike those heaped on Moleskines. Miquelrius has smooth pages wrapped in a flexible, leatherlike cover. These notebooks are a bit less expensive than Moleskines.

You'll find dozens of other choices to fit your likes and budget. Design guru Bruce Mau favors spiral notebooks like those we lugged around in high school. "I'm not picky about the brand," he says. "I should be more aesthetic about them, but I'm not."

"I made three neat stacks of my 'Paris' notebooks. In France these notebooks are known as *carnets moleskins*; 'moleskin', in this case, being its black oilcloth binding... I wrote my name and address on the front page, offering a reward to the finder."

—Bruce Chatwin,
The Songlines

got enough PENCILS?

When inspiration strikes at home, Susan Polis Schutz, co-founder of Blue Mountain Arts greeting cards, is ready. A built-in hardwood wall rack holds five rows of finely sharpened colored pencils. The large rack serves as colorful artwork, and Schutz and husband Stephen can quickly reach for pencils when they have ideas.

Think of ways you can display pencils, pens or markers to have them handy when inspiration strikes.

BECOME A
CARD SHARK.

Index cards are the darlings of the pocket-protector crowd, offering endless opportunities for filing systems, color coding and the Dewey Decimal System.

BUT MANY CREATIVE PEOPLE ALSO RAVE ABOUT INDEX CARDS.

For certain projects, they work great. And it's inspiring to shuffle idea-filled cards around on a table, detecting patterns and making connections.

"I have index cards and pens all over the house—by the bed, in the bathroom, in the kitchen, by the phones, and I have them in the glove compartment of my car... whenever I am leaving the house without my purse—in which there are actual notepads, let alone index cards—I fold an index card lengthwise in half, stick it in my back pocket along with a pen and head out, knowing that if I have an idea, or see something lovely or strange or for any reason worth remembering, I will be able to jot down a couple of words to remind me of it."

—Anne Lamott,
Bird by Bird:
Some instructions
on writing and life

"I never travel without my notebook. One should always have something sensational to read in the train."

—Oscar Wilde

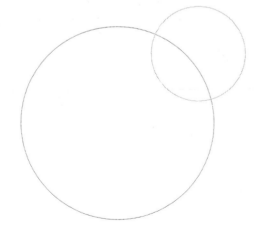

note taking IN A
DIGITAL WORLD.

Though handcuffed to my iMac and PowerBook, I've never found the romance of using computers for note taking. Paper notebooks serve me well.

But like most creative people I've talked with, I do use computers as databases for ideas first captured on paper. And I know a few creative souls who are totally paper-free note takers. They claim to love it—especially those with PDAs.

Lots of software firms promise grand results with their note-related products.

NoteTaker software for Mac users is a note and idea organizer—its interface uses "spiral" notebook pages with section tabs. For PC users, Microsoft OneNote lets users record, organize and share notes.

A software called ndxCards is a digital version of index cards. The software helps users organize freeform note cards using subjects and keywords. And a note-gathering program called TreePad mimics the tree-branch or mind-map approach.

THERE ARE DOZENS MORE. ASK AROUND OR TEST DOWNLOADS TO SEE IF YOUR WORK AND LIFESTYLE MATCH UP WITH DIGITAL NOTE TAKING.

8

YOUR YARD ISN'T THE
ONLY YARD IN TOWN.

and your next idea
MAY BE JUST OVER THE FENCE.

"begin with another's to END WITH YOUR OWN."

—Baltasar Gracian, PHILOSOPHER

THERE'S AN IDEA OUT THERE.

Maybe you'll spot it by seeing how others tackle problems and find solutions.

In the 1950s, fast-food restaurants added drive-through lanes to serve car-loving customers. Banks and dry-cleaners soon borrowed the idea.

Today, all types of businesses use drive-throughs. The Little White Wedding Chapel in Las Vegas offers drive-through ceremonies. Loma Linda Medical Center gives flu shots while patients sit in cars. Seigl's Lumber Yard has drive-through lanes for tools and materials.

The hypercarbon now used in tennis rackets was first developed to stabilize satellites. Home smoke detectors and scratch-resistant lenses also stemmed from space-industry applications.

STUMPED? INVESTIGATE CREATIVE SOLUTIONS OF OTHER INDUSTRIES.

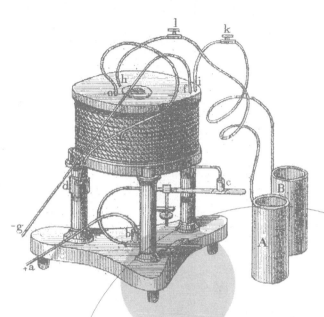

SEE A SOLUTION, suck it up.

In 1900, London's Empire Music Hall displayed a dust-removing machine. Only one problem: It didn't remove dust. Instead, the unit blasted out compressed air, which just sort of blew dust particles about the floor.

Hubert Cecil Booth took one look and spotted an idea. He built a similar machine based on suction and patented the first vacuum.

SEE WHAT YOU CAN *borrow.*

List three innovative brands or disciplines unlike your own:

1.

2.

3.

EXPLORE THEIR PROBLEM-SOLVING METHODS. WHAT CAN YOU USE?

usufruct: *n.* The right to use and enjoy the profits and advantages belonging to another as long as their own property is not damaged or altered in any way.

CREATIVE BORROWING HAS A

rich heritage.

Mozart borrowed from Bach to compose concertos.

Seventeenth-century French musicians borrowed from military music of ancient Greece and Turkey.

Poussin's The Crossing of the Red Sea borrowed from Myron's Discus Thrower.

Paul Simon borrowed from South African musicians to create *Graceland*. The Rolling Stones borrowed from B.B. King and Solomon Burke.

IN ALL CREATIVE FIELDS, BORROWING BRINGS ON BOUNTY.

borrowing
CAFFEINATES IDEAS.

"Our Coffee Master booklets were inspired by old book covers, travel journals and end papers," says Doug Keyes, senior designer with Starbucks Creative Group. "And real passports inspired the Coffee Passports used by employees to document their coffee-tasting 'journeys.'"

EXPLORE THE MASTERS
for material.

When artist Willem de Kooning came to America in the 1920s, he met a young painter, Arshile Gorky.

Lacking formal training, Gorky learned classical techniques by trying to recreate masterpieces. De Kooning was impressed and borrowed the process.

Years later de Kooning talked of using Rubens in his own work, fusing classical and modern into a new form.

What masters of innovation do you admire? Edison or Einstein? Curie or Carver? Picasso or Pavlov? Dali or Disney?

WHO INSPIRES YOU? INSPECT THEIR LIVES, METHODS, IDEAS.

"Masters open the door, but it's up to you to enter."

—Chinese proverb

LIST IDEA MASTERS YOU ADMIRE:

1.

2.

3.

4.

5.

EXPLORE THEIR METHODS.
SEE WHAT YOU CAN BORROW.

LIFE IMITATES ART,
art imitates life.

Film director James Brooks needed visual ideas for a pool scene in *Spanglish*. He found them in artwork hanging on his wall.

The D.J. Hall painting captures a type of upscale West Coast woman, said Brooks, much like the character played by Tea Leoni in *Spanglish*. In the movie, Leoni actually wears the shirt Ms. Hall's model wore, and the set includes the painting's banana plants and African lilies.

AND AS ART INSPIRES FILMMAKERS, FILM INSPIRES DESIGNERS.

Watching *Something's Gotta Give*, David DeMattei, designer for Williams-Sonoma Home, admired several upholstered headboards used in the film. Inspired, DeMattei created five headboard designs for the Home collection.

GO BEHIND THE CURTAINS AND BORROW FROM:

1. Films
2. Plays
3. Concerts
4. Dance
5. Sports

"Originality consists of the achievement of new combinations and not of the creation of something out of nothing."

—Richard V. Clemence,
ECONOMIST AND WRITER

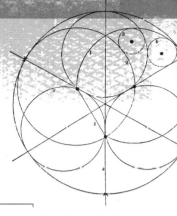

HOW LEFTOVERS
heated up A PRODUCT PACKAGE.

Where do you find ideas for something as commonplace as aluminum foil?

Mark Nielsen, an in-house designer for Publix Super Markets, faced that question when asked to create packaging for the chain's brand of aluminum foil.

He remembered a night at a Japanese steakhouse.

"A waiter wrapped our leftovers in foil, then made sculptures of the containers," he said. "One looked like Green Goblin from *Spider-Man*. Another was shaped like a rose."

NIELSEN SPOTTED AN IDEA.

"I started thinking that there's no reason foil sculptures have to be only for leftovers," he says. "Why not make them for the heck of it? And that's what I began doing."

He created hand-size elephants and moose, alligators and turtles. He then photographed these shiny creatures and gave them prominent positions on boxes of foil.

The result? Fun, eye-grabbing packages for an everyday product.

Who provides you with imaginative, energetic service?
Explore their ideas and techniques—what can you borrow?

RESTAURANTS	HOTELS	RETAILERS	OTHERS

BORROWING HELPS
BAG BEARD AWARDS.

AvroKO, a celebrated group of New York architects and designers, knows the genius of borrowing. Especially after capturing James Beard Awards for creative restaurant design.

Designing the Stanton Social restaurant, AvroKO paid tribute to the Manhattan neighborhood's garment history.

A backlit wine wall was inspired by herringbone fabric. Banquette pillows have leather straps mimicking men's suspenders. Lamp shades borrow from the curved patterns of old-fashioned girdles.

AvroKO peers over many fences for inspiration. For Sapa restaurant, its designers studied a Vietnamese mountaintop village where France's wealthy vacationed in the 1800s. Wire lanterns, casement windows and garden urns give Sapa an Asian and Parisian ambiance.

For Public restaurant, AvroKO turned to municipal buildings from the 1930s. Décor includes bronze post-office boxes, restroom doors with mail slots and menus made from government forms.

THREE MORE PLACES TO LOOK FOR IDEAS:

1. FASHION—CONSIDER FORGOTTEN STYLES.

2. RESORTS—BYPASS TODAY'S HOT SPOTS AND LOOK BACK.

3. ARCHITECTURE—EXPLORE ERAS AND INDUSTRIES.

DON'T BE A NIHilist.

A nihilist—when lower case—thinks nothing has real existence.

A **NIH**ilist thinks nothing exists except that created by his own mind or company—a disciple of the **N**ot **I**nvented **H**ere philosophy.

Not Invented Here held a smidgen of legitimacy in days of vast research labs filled with engineers at IBM, P&G and other mega firms.

BUT THAT ERA HAS ENDED.

More than a quarter of P&G's innovations now come from outside sources. IBM depends on strategic partnerships. Even self-reliant Apple now joins hands with Hewlett-Packard and Motorola.

And products from one industry inspire ideas in another industry.

Electric toothbrushes inspired Dawn Power Dish Brush. Ballpoint pens inspired Clorox Whitening Pen. Listerine PocketPaks inspired Hartz Dental Breath Strips for Dogs.

WALK AWAY FROM NOT INVENTED HERE.

LAUNDRY SPOTS.

Sherwin-Williams turned to laundry soap containers when designing Dutch Boy Twist and Pour paint delivery system. And Purina looked to the laundry room when creating Kibbles pour-top.

INVENTED AT YOUR PLACE	INVENTED AT THEIR PLACES
old ideas	tried and proven methods and designs
existing ideas	
inchoate ideas	

FRESH SOLUTIONS

Of course we all have our lim-
its, but how can you possibly
find your boundaries unless
you explore as far and wide as
you can?"

—A.E. Hotchner,
NOVELIST AND BIOGRAPHER

TREATMENTS TO
KICK THE **NIH**ilistic HABIT.

TREATMENT ONE: *go cold turkey*

Flush these statements:
"We don't do it that way."
"We don't care what anybody else is doing."
"We have all the answers right here."
"It won't work."

TREATMENT TWO: *learn new habits*

Go online or to a library. Find trade magazines
for six unrelated professions and industries.

1.

2.

3.

4.

5.

6.

Subscribe. Read. Spot ideas.

TREATMENT THREE: *find new playgrounds*

Take a day away from your workplace. Visit retailers and
supermarkets. List or purchase at least six clever and useful products.

1.

2.

3.

4.

5.

6.

Take the list and purchases to work the next day.
Brainstorm on how the products might inspire ideas and offer solutions.

call in *cavalry,*
SEND OUT SCOUTS.

I know of a brand communications firm that sends out its people on quarterly scavenger hunts for off-the-wall products and offbeat publications.

Cirque du Soleil calls in teachers to give workshops on anything and everything to its dancers, acrobats, musicians and other performers.

Are you asking people in and sending people out?

How can you call in the cavalry to boost creativity? Ask a theater director to give a workshop on acting methods. Have an improv company teach techniques for spontaneity. Hire a chef to give a cooking class.

How can you send out your team to scout ideas? Check the local papers for exhibits, lectures and gallery openings. Dispatch the troops.

WORK ALONE? Convert these suggestions into a personal action plan. Take classes, visit museums, attend lectures, cook recipes, network with peers.

break FROM YOUR FUNK.

For years, the Funk Brothers backed up Marvin Gaye, the Temptations and other Motown greats. At night, the Funk Brothers refined their signature sound by prowling and playing Detroit's jazz clubs. The next morning, they would bring ideas back into the Snake Pit studio, adding jazz voicings and thick textures to their arrangements.

get out OF YOUR CUBE.

To find ideas and avoid Not Invented Here syndrome, Hallmark Cards opens its doors to outside influences.

"We get our people out of cubes and into cities," says Scott Orazem, director of design studios.

CITY TOURS.
Hallmark designers, writers and photographers regularly tour metropolitan areas. "These trips are purely for renewal and inspiration," says Mark Spencer, program director.

On a Chicago tour, participants explored museums and architecture, art fairs and retailers. They dined at new restaurants and hit shows at Steppenwolf Theater. In Washington, the Hallmark group studied history and politics, theater and art. And the Santa Fe group visited art colonies and focused on Native American culture.

"People return with strong inspiration," says Spencer. "For example, one designer created gift wrap inspired by theater costumes she admired in Chicago."

IN-HOUSE GALLERY.
In addition to going out into the world, Hallmark brings the world in. A headquarters gallery hosts ten shows a year. Recent exhibitions focused on watercolors, embroidered fabric and antique furniture.

"People from throughout the company visit for inspiration," says Spencer.

LECTURE SERIES.
Hallmark also hosts in-house lectures, pulling in creative experts to share their works and experiences. Recent guests include poets, book designers and poster printers.

"We seek ways to open our minds," says Orazem. "We engage with people outside our world to exchange ideas."

HOW ARE YOU OPENING DOORS AND MINDS?

THE WORLD IS WAITING.
CHECK IT OUT, BRING IT IN.

CITY TOURS

Visit galleries and museums, restaurants and retailers. Start with your own city. Then stretch into other metropolitan areas.

What tours can you take?

GALLERY SPACE

Organize a gallery in your workspace—even if it's a vacant storage room, neglected corner or hallway wall. Invite artists and craftspeople to exhibit their works. Work alone or in a three-person shop? No sweat. Subscribe to arts and crafts publications. Clip out photos and tape to a blank wall. From time to time, add pottery, jewelry and other art to your collection.

How will your gallery look?

LECTURES AND WORKSHOPS

Invite designers, writers, artists, photographers and other craftspeople to talk with your team. Have them show work in your gallery. If you work solo or part of a small team, scan your newspaper's entertainment and lifestyle sections for coming events. Attend lectures, workshops and documentaries.

What speakers will you invite? What events will you attend?

9

WHO YOU
GONNA CALL?

build your
NETWORK.

Philip Johnson held leisurely dinners at the Century Club to exchange ideas with other architects.

As a Marketing 50 member, Judy Verses of Verizon meets monthly to share ideas with forty-nine other marketing officers of global companies.

At Georgia State University's Marketing Roundtable, members pay $5,000 each to swap ideas.

CREATIVE PEOPLE NETWORK.
BECAUSE NETWORKING WORKS.

"Networking is a powerful way to stay alert and gather insights," says Hallmark's Scott Orazem. "I reach out to people who have similar roles in other industries."

Jeff Wilson, president of Midwest of Cannon Falls, networks with top retailers across the country. "They provide quick pulse-taking on what's happening in terms of trends and needs," he says.

Many creative people find networks in professional groups such as AIGA, American Marketing Association, Public Relations Society of America and International Association of Business Communicators.

"My most relevant networking is through InSource," says Tim Cox, Publix's director of creative services. "It's a great way for an in-house creative director like me to exchange ideas with other in-house managers."

Creative people frequently network through conventions and workshops, such as the TED, HOW or Gel conferences. Others use online chat rooms and communities, such as the HOW Forum (www.howdesign.com).

And others simply pull together their own informal networks, seeking out people they respect and with whom they have simpatico relationships.

"I go out of my way to surround myself with people who are much smarter than I am," says Erin Whelan of *Real Simple* magazine. "I appreciate them so much because they enhance and broaden my views."

DON'T GO IT ALONE.
NETWORK.

HOW ONE FIRM'S NETWORK
SEES INTO THE FUTURE.

With clients like Absolut, Diet Coke and Balducci's, Pearlfisher needs to visualize future trends. Networking provides the crystal ball.

The design and branding firm maintains a robust network of opinion shapers on both sides of the Atlantic. Insights pour into its LifeModes process for exploring topics like luxury, taste, and nightlife.

"In all cultures, there are inner-directed tribes and outer-directed tribes," says Mark Rodgers, insight director. Inner-directed tribes typically seek guidance from inside themselves rather than from the thoughts and opinions of others.

"To find trends and ideas," Rodgers says, "we look to inner-directed tribespeople. These are the change agents."

Pearlfisher's network examines the fringes—what's on the verge of becoming a trend.

"There's an ocean bed of basic needs," says Claire Hyland, insight manager, "but waves of cultural changes rise above those beds. It's those waves we explore."

DOES YOUR NETWORK INCLUDE VISIONARIES?

"The future is here. It's just
not widely distributed yet."

—William Gibson,
SCIENCE FICTION WRITER

SIX NETWORKING
nuggets.

1. PICK STRONG PARTNERS.

Just because you hit it off with a person doesn't necessarily mean she fits your network. Likewise, don't select a person only because he's bright. If the chemistry's lacking, you can forget about sharing.

2. BE A STRONG PARTNER.

Nothing murders networking faster than all take, no give. Be a team player. Don't be stingy with insights and ideas.

3. FOCUS ON WHAT'S IMPORTANT.

With all the networking options, it's easy to spread yourself thin. Decide your needs upfront, and make sure your networks satisfy those goals.

4. EXPOSE YOURSELF.

Be available to partners. Answer phone calls and e-mails. Meet when you say you'll meet. Do what you say you'll do.

5. REMEMBER ETHOS.

All relationships—including networks—are built on the three steps of knowing, liking and trusting. Let partners know you. Be a person they like being around. Build trust.

6. NURTURE THE NETWORK.

Pay attention to personal stuff. Send cards and notes. Distribute articles and reprints. Keep partners alert to good books and key events. Stay plugged in.

"Keep away from people who try to belittle your ambitions. Small people always do that, but the really great make you feel that you, too, can become great."

—Mark Twain

networking WORKSHEET

List entities or people in each category. Decide what meets your goals.

PROFESSIONAL ORGANIZATIONS

PROFESSIONAL NETWORKING GROUPS

ONLINE FORUMS, CHAT ROOMS, COMMUNITIES, LISTSERVS

CONFERENCES, CONVENTIONS, WORKSHOPS, ROUNDTABLES

SELF-ORGANIZED NETWORKS, POSSIBLE CANDIDATES

10

WE'VE ALL HAD OUR SHARE OF
BLUNDERS, FLOPS, BAD MOVES,
GOOFS, GAFFES, CLUNKERS.

SPOT WHAT YOU CAN DO

to salvage them.

MILK MISTAKES
FOR ALL THEY'RE WORTH.

I've been involved in projects that couldn't have gone more wrong without loss of life. But good things came from those disasters when I reloaded and tried again.

EVERYBODY FAILS FROM TIME TO TIME.

The Wright brothers crashed before Kitty Hawk. Lincoln blew two Senate elections. Disney's first cartoon company went belly-up.

There's New Coke. The Edsel. A record player with a turntable that Chrysler added to luxury cars in the 1950s. Skip city.

And there's the fellow who invented an airtight casket to keep out insects. He didn't consider methane gas produced by decaying bodies. Talk about a product explosion.

But these people and companies learned from their mistakes. By exploring failures, they generated better and bigger ideas.

reshape MISTAKES.

Lush Cosmetics created Solid Gold Bath, a bubble-bath loaf. Its stores displayed the loaves on large bread racks—which turned out to be a mistake. Customers had to wait around for an employee to pull down the loaf and slice off a piece. Sales suffered. Lush learned from the mistake and re-packaged the product in sausage shapes. Stores stacked them in crates, making the product easy to grab. Sales surged.

you must
BE MISTAKEN.

BITE THE BULLET AND LIST THREE OF
YOUR MISTAKES OR FAILURES:

1.

2.

3.

How can you convert these into better ideas?

From error to error, one
discovers the entire truth."
—Sigmund Freud

MAKE good mistakes
AND WORK THEM OVER.

GOOD MISTAKES HAVE STRONG EFFORTS BUT SEEMINGLY BAD RESULTS.

Bad mistakes have sloppy, mediocre efforts and bad results.

Thomas Edison explored hundreds of good mistakes on the way to making a light bulb. John Pemberton explored his good miss at health tonic and gave us Coca-Cola. Arthur Fry explored the good mistake of a weak glue and brought about Post-its.

Roy Plunkett mistakenly left chlorofluorocarbons on his radiator. Big mess. He explored his good mistake and came up with Teflon.

Tom Watson told IBM employees to double mistakes to improve success rates. You better believe he was talking about good mistakes.

BE WILLING TO MAKE GOOD MISTAKES. AND TRY MAKING THEM EARLY. WHILE THEY'RE STILL CHEAP.

"The person who is afraid to make mistakes will be afraid to try."

—Arthur Combs,
EDUCATIONAL PSYCHOLOGIST

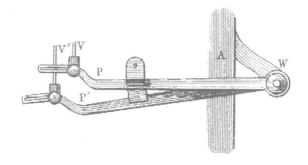

"I knew a man who grabbed a cat by the tail and learned 40 percent more about cats than the man who didn't."

—Mark Twain

A MISTAKE SPOTTED OVER THERE
IS AN IDEA SIZZLING OVER HERE.

A Texas concert hall owes its acoustics to a New York mistake.

During a photo shoot at Carnegie Hall in the 1940s, the ceiling was revamped to accommodate extra lighting. By mistake, architects created an open area in the ceiling. They later discovered the bonus space actually enriched sound from the stage.

Jaffe Holden Acoustics embraced Carnegie's mistake when designing Bass Performance Hall in Fort Worth, Texas. A 45-foot opening above the stage reverberates and blends the music, releasing it as full-tone sound.

"Learn from the mistakes of others. You can never live long enough to make them all yourself."

—John Luther, WRITER

BORROW SOMEBODY'S SCREW-UP.

In this box, record a mistake you've spotted
or read about.

In these boxes, write ways you can convert
the mistake into a good idea for yourself.

look around—
EVERYBODY'S MAKING MISTAKES.

MISTAKES TOURISTS MAKE.
1. Packing too much.
2. Outdated guidebooks.
3. Too many reservations.

MISTAKES PARENTS MAKE.
1. Inconsistent rules.
2. Talking too much.
3. Words not matching actions.

MISTAKES SPEAKERS MAKE.
1. Speaking without passion.
2. Reading speech word for word.
3. Failing to prepare.

MISTAKES WEB DESIGNERS MAKE.
1. Confusing web design with magic tricks.
2. Too much material on one page.
3. Navigational failures.

MISTAKES COMIC STORE OWNERS MAKE.
1. Opening with little capital.
2. Not paying taxes.
3. Being a collector.

MISTAKES FILM DIRECTORS MAKE.
1. Giving emotional directions.
2. Applying style without reason.
3. Neglecting the audience.

MISTAKES TAXPAYERS MAKE.
1. Poor math.
2. Losing receipts.
3. Forgetting about interest.

MISTAKES DIETERS MAKE.
1. Eliminating fruit.
2. Splurging away from home.
3. Not exercising regularly.

MISTAKES HOMEBUYERS MAKE.
1. Choosing poor location.
2. Buying for curb appeal.
3. Not having inspection.

MISTAKES SALESPEOPLE MAKE.
1. Not knowing buyer.
2. Talking too much.
3. No emotional connection.

MISTAKES MARATHON TRAINEES MAKE.
1. Increasing mileage too quickly.
2. Ignoring injuries.
3. Not stretching enough.

MISTAKES NEW DOG OWNERS MAKE.
1. Not researching desired dogs.
2. Not understanding commitment.
3. Not training properly.

11

FINDERS,

keepers.

BE A CREATIVE
street scavenger.

Pick up that piece of litter—even if it belongs to someone else. Especially if it belongs to someone else. Because that crumpled ticket, handbill or list might unfold as your next idea.

Found objects make up the signature style of American artist Robert Rauschenberg. His *Rebus* blends comic strips, election posters and a child's drawings. *First Landing Jump* includes a tire, torn shirt and working light bulb.

Clearly the first artist to glorify found objects was Marcel Duchamp, an accomplished painter. A century ago, he nailed a tossed-aside coat rack to the floor and called it *Trebuchet*, or trap. He spent the next several years finding objects and placing them in new settings.

Duchamp and other Dada movement artists believed people changed their perceptions by looking at everyday objects in new ways.

AND WHEN YOU CHANGE PERCEPTIONS, YOU CHANGE YOUR VIEWS OF THE WORLD.

objet trouvé: *n.* A natural object
or an artifact not originally intended as art,
found and considered to have aesthetic value.

"THE ARTIST IS A RECEPTACLE
for emotions that come from all over the place."

—Pablo Picasso

Picasso understood the magic of ephemera and transformed it into art forms. As early as 1912, he and Georges Braque included objects such as discarded wallpaper and chair caning in collages.

Picasso also used found items for his sculptures. A famous example is Baboon and Young, a 21-inch piece popular with both adults and children.

Two toy cars became the baboon's head. For its plump body, Picasso used a jug, adding handles from other pots to create shoulders.

Picasso created Baboon and Young in 1951 and four years later cast six bronze sculptures from the original. New York's Museum of Modern Art displays the fifth casting of bronze.

"The artist is a receptacle for emotions that come from all over the place; from the sky, from the earth, from a scrap of paper, from a passing shape, from a spider's web."

—Pablo Picasso

"Kant proposed that our understanding is not simply a reflection of the objective world around us, but it also constitutes this world. It is not that objects simply speak to us; they also conform to our ways of knowing. The mind thus is an active process of forming and re-forming the world."

—Rollo May, EXISTENTIAL PSYCHOLOGIST

Everybody's
TALKING TRASH.

MORE AND MORE PEOPLE ARE FINDING IDEAS IN FOUND OBJECTS.

"Piled in my workspace right now are small bars of soap I've found while traveling," says Kristy Moore, art director at *Martha Stewart Living.* "I get inspired by the packaging, the soft colors and the way words are etched in the surfaces."

Starbucks designers collect found objects on their travels to coffee farms in Europe and Latin America as well as closer to home. "This ephemera includes passport stamps, postcards, bits of type, ticket stubs, weathered wood and dozens of other things," says Doug Keyes, Starbucks senior designer.

And Gail Anderson, *Rolling Stone* alumna and now SpotCo's art director, finds ideas in salt-and-pepper shakers and bottle caps gathered through the years.

"I've also swiped typography from old matchbooks, tobacco tins and crate labels," she says.

"There could be something amazing nestled in the pile of debris on the sidewalk in front of your office... So what if that catalog cover sparked from seeing a wad of trampled pink bubble gum on the steely gray asphalt."

—Glen Helfand, WRITER

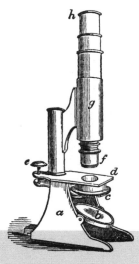

found ON YOUR NEWSSTAND.

There's even a magazine devoted to found objects. *Found* is filled with finds of readers and fans—love letters, birthday cards, kids' homework, to-do lists, phone bills, doodles on napkins, photos and much more. Check newsstands or www.foundmagazine.com.

HOW A *found object* MADE A BIG BANG.

LISA GREENBERG IS A BIG FAN OF FOUND OBJECTS.

"I find inspiration in everything," says the associate creative director at GJP Advertising. "My bookshelves are jammed with every object you can imagine."

So when time came to create a holiday self-promotion, Greenberg reached in her piles and pulled out bubble wrap.

"It's impossible to resist popping the stuff," she says. "I've always wanted to use it in a promotion."

GJP's Go Out With A Bang calendar uses bubble wrap for counting down to the New Year. Each bubble is numbered so recipients pop off a day at a time. An enclosure lists thirty-one ways to go out with a bang.

Lisa is already thinking about next year's card. And she'll likely spot the idea in her found objects.

"I get ideas from street merchandise, seashells, broken toys, you name it," she says. "Right now I'm having a space-age moment."

WHERE'S YOUR COLLECTION? ARE YOU ADDING TO IT AND SIFTING THROUGH IT?

lost and found DEPARTMENT

Find four or five simple objects—on streets
or in drawers. Place in different settings. Play
with them. Take them apart. Combine them.
Let them point you toward ideas.

WHERE IN THE WORLD
did you find THAT?

FOUND BY LIBRARIANS IN RETURNED BOOKS
wedding pictures
surgical clamp
Kleenex (clean and used)
rubber snake
Kool-Aid packet

FOUND BY R.L. CAGLE WHILE BICYCLING
ON A COUNTRY ROAD IN ILLINOIS
one bottle Jack Daniels, empty
one Trojan Shared Sensation condom, unopened
one package, EPT Early Pregnancy Test, opened

FOUND AT DISNEY WORLD
*(The park's lost and found
department tags about one
thousand items a day.)*
toupees and wigs
engagement rings
sunglasses and caps
passports
masks

FOUND DURING LAST YEAR'S
GREAT AMERICAN CLEANUP
commode seat
arrowhead
doll's head
taped diaper stuffed with fruit
accordion

**FOUND ON VIRGINIA'S BEACHES DURING
INTERNATIONAL COASTAL CLEANUP**
piece of NASA rocket
bowling ball
bottle with letter inside
boxer shorts
flyswatter

BOOKS FOUND ON NEW YORK SUBWAYS
The Lord of the Flies
The Firefighter's Workout Book
Life in a Mediaeval Monastery
How to Meet the Right Woman
The Glucose Revolution
textbooks (mostly math)
Bibles

12

LOOK FOR ONE THING,

stumble OVER ANOTHER.

BE ON ALERT

FOR *serendipity*.

Exploring often brings about serendipity—the spotting of ideas totally unrelated to what you went searching for.

One fine summer day George Ballas pulled into a car wash looking for a cleaner automobile. But he exited with the idea for a lawn product.

Serendipity hit as Ballas watched spinning nylon bristles scrub his car. He rushed home, punched holes in a can and inserted fishing line. Then he removed his lawn edger's blade and attached the can.

WEED EATER WAS BORN.

Sir Alexander Fleming spotted penicillin while actually exploring staphylococcus bacteria. Wilhelm Röntgen spotted X-rays while exploring cathode rays. James Wright spotted Silly Putty while exploring silicone substitutes for rubber.

WANT SERENDIPITY'S SURGE? STAY ALERT.

soft focus EXERCISE.

Practice peripheral awareness.
Set your gaze on an object.
Keep a soft focus on the spot,
expanding awareness to the
edges of your visual field. As you
do this exercise, you'll also find
your body relaxes and your mind
becomes quieter.

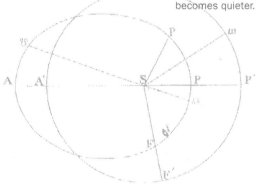

DOES SERENDIPITY WORK?
ask the wizard.

Frank Baum imagined a Kansas girl being swept by tornado to a faraway land where she meets a wizard. But Baum needed a title for his tale.

SERENDIPITY STRUCK ONE AFTERNOON AS HE WAS FILING PAPERWORK.

"My gaze was caught by the gilt letters on the three drawers of the file cabinet," Baum later wrote. "The first was A-G. The next drawer was labeled H-N. And on the last were the letters O-Z. *The Wizard of Oz* it at once became."

Contemporary author Katy Gibbons experienced similar serendipity. While writing about three generations of women during World War II, Gibbons used the working title of *Eagle Avenue*. But she knew her editor would insist on a more alluring title.

Just before submitting her manuscript, Gibbons was flipping through a book on antique folk medicines. She stumbled across a list of various remedies, or "charms," as they are known—charms for headaches, charms for stomach problems, charms for relaxation.

Gibbons' eyes came to rest on one particularly enticing charm. And at that moment *Charms for the Easy Life* became her book's fitting and memorable title.

Shuffling through paperwork? Thumbing through books? Switch off automatic pilot—serendipity could be in your hands.

"You don't reach Serendip by plotting a course for it. You have to set out in good faith for elsewhere and lose your bearings serendipitously."

—John Barth,
   The Last Voyage of
   Somebody the Sailor

MAKE DISCOVERIES
by *accident and sagacity.*

The word serendipity was coined by Sir Horace Walpole in reference to a Persian fairy tale called *The Three Princes of Serendip.*

In the story, three highly educated siblings are sent on a journey by their father, the king of Serendip. During their adventures, the young princes make "discoveries by accident and sagacity, of things they were not in quest of."

Serendip was the ancient name for Ceylon, now called Sri Lanka. *The Three Princes of Serendip* was popular with sixteenth-century Venetian intellectuals who entertained each other with riddles and fables.

HOW SERENDIPITY
SAVED THE BALL.

The Costume Institute Ball was days away, and David Monn couldn't find chairs.

This was Monn's first time designing Metropolitan Museum of Art's celebrity-filled event and everything else was falling into place. Seven thousand gardenias had arrived by chartered jet. Belgian linen tablecloths were starched and pressed. Topiaries waited in refrigerated trucks.

BUT NO CHAIRS.

Monn had his heart set on slatted green chairs like those clustered around fountains in Luxembourg Gardens. But he had phoned every supplier in New York, and such chairs couldn't be found.

THEN SERENDIPITY HIT.

Monn had grabbed a cab on Fifth Avenue, heading for an unrelated appointment. Traffic inched along, and Monn's taxi came to a standstill in front of Bryant Park. Monn gazed out the window and couldn't believe his eyes. There in the park, scattered across lawns and walkways, were hundreds of slatted green chairs.

Monn borrowed the chairs. The ball was a bash. Serendipity strikes again.

Stay aware—in taxis, on sidewalks and at airports.

YOUR IDEA MAY BE WHERE YOU LEAST EXPECT IT.

13

COLLABORATE
WITH A *hibiscus.*

"KEEP EYES OPEN TO WHAT
Mother Nature has to teach."

—George Washington Carver

Monet's *Water Lilies*. Weston's *Pepper No. 30*. O'Keefe's *Cow's Skull with Calico Roses*.

NATURE INSPIRES IDEAS.

And when it comes to fully embracing nature's influences, the crown of roses goes to Leonardo da Vinci. His observation of animals and landscapes resulted in remarkably realistic paintings. His study of anatomy led to accurately proportioned figures.

Nature became his studio. He sketched how animals looked far away and close-up. He made notes on differences in plants under midday sun and evening shadows. He recognized before others that "the sun does not move."

He was fascinated by water's paradoxes: "...it is warm and is cold, carries away or sets down, hollows out or builds up, tears or establishes, fills or empties, speeds or is still..."

By watching water, da Vinci created plans for locks and canals. He sketched machines for excavating waterways and imagined a navigable channel linking Florence to the sea.

WHAT'S NATURE SHOWING YOU?

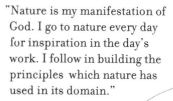

"Nature is my manifestation of God. I go to nature every day for inspiration in the day's work. I follow in building the principles which nature has used in its domain."

—Frank Lloyd Wright

BUILD THE WAY
nature builds.

Frank Lloyd Wright, arguably America's greatest architect, designed more than 1,000 works and created furniture and lamps, tableware and art glass.

Nature inspired Wright's creativity. Its influence began during summers spent on his uncle's farm as a boy. There he first explored nature's patterns and rhythms—outcroppings of rocks, shifting sandbars, the cantilever properties of tree branches.

Wright constantly collaborated with nature to design masterpieces. His earth-hugging prairie houses. His sky-lighted forest of columns in the Johnson Wax headquarters. His cascading cantilevers in the famous Fallingwater house.

"Study nature, love nature, stay close to nature," Wright told his apprentices. "Nature will never fail you."

Learn more about Wright's reliance on nature. Read related books. Watch Ken Burns' documentary. Visit pertinent web sites. Tour Wright's buildings. (Find a public site list at www.franklloydwright.org.)

biomimetics: *n.* The study of biological processes and nature for methods and ideas. To mimic biology and nature.

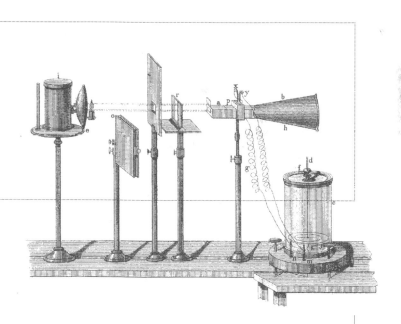

TAKE A HIKE
AND TAKE NOTICE.

Diane von Furstenberg loves hiking. And she loves taking discoveries from those hikes back to work.

The fashion designer gathers or photographs leaves, stones and sticks. Then she uses these objects to inspire fabric designs.

FASHION AND HOME DESIGNERS FREQUENTLY BORROW FROM NATURE.

Plants offer color schemes—red berries next to green holly leaves, mauve crocus bulbs accented by the bold yellow of its stamens. Trees provide toning ideas—shades of leaves, bark and vines.

Beaches show palettes of harmony—pastiches of sand, driftwood and sea oats.

Stones, seeds, fruits, vegetables, fur, snow, streams, rainfall and sunsets—all help designers spot ideas for colors and textures, shapes and tones.

ARE YOU TAKING NATURE TO WORK?

walk OUT.

Don't let the technical blind you from the natural. List three places you can walk this week to look for ideas in nature.

1.

2.

3.

STACK twigs.

NATURE DOESN'T JUST INSPIRE ANDY GOLDSWORTHY. IT'S HIS CANVAS.

The Scotsman roams forests and shorelines, making ephemeral sculptures from whatever catches his eye: bits of ice, reeds and thorns, rocks and twigs.

When he's completed a piece of earth art, he takes one photo.

THEN HE LEAVES THE PIECE BEHIND.

To learn more about Goldsworthy's art, take a look at his books: *Wood* and *Stone*. Or watch the documentary *Rivers and Tides*.

"When I work with a leaf, rock, stick, it is not just that material in itself, it is an opening into the process of life within and around it."

—Andy Goldsworthy,
SCULPTOR

create EARTH ART.

Use Andy Goldsworthy's process to boost
your creativity. Walk in nature and make earth
art—an arrangement of twigs, a stack of
pebbles, a grouping of leaves. These small
acts of art will fire creative neurons—and
you'll likely generate other ideas as a result.

jawbones TO JEWELS.

Artist GoGo Ferguson casts natural patterns into elegant gold and silver jewelry. Among Ferguson's creations are necklaces inspired by scallop shells, rattlesnake jawbones, armadillo sternums and shark vertebrae. "What most people step over on the tide line, I see in a completely different light," she says. "You can't improve on nature's designs." See her work at www.gogojewelry.com.

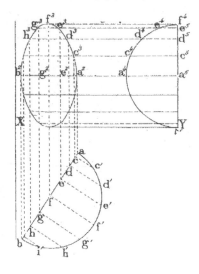

HOW MUSSELS
HELPED MAKE GLUE.

Kaichang Li stood idly at the ocean's edge, watching waves crash against mussels attached to nearby rocks. The Oregon State University professor wondered how the mollusks held on.

Li had cause to ponder, being an expert in adhesives. He decided to take a closer look at the mussels' byssus—small threads that attach to rocks.

"I knew of no other type of adhesive that could work this well in water and withstand so much force," says Li.

Analyzing the threads in his lab, Li found an unusual protein composition provided a water-resistant adhesive. He saw potential for wood glue. Only one problem: Mussel protein isn't readily available.

His solution came during lunch months later, when Li thought about how soybeans provide abundant, cheap protein. By adding amino acids to soy protein, Li's team developed water-resistant, environmentally safe wood adhesives.

All this because Kaichang Li checked out mussels near his ocean home.

WHAT'S OUTSIDE YOUR DOOR?

"There are millions of years of research in nature that can help us... enormous opportunities exist for people to make discoveries and transform these into successful patents."

—Anja-Karina Pahl,
CONFERENCE ORGANIZER,
International Biomimetics

HOW A FLY AIDED
a hearing aid.

That buzzing insect might guide you to an idea.

That's what happened with Ron Miles, a Binghamton University nanotechnologist who is replicating fly ears for hearing aids.

Most flies don't even have ears. But the Ormia fly does—and they're powerful little buggers. Ormia ears pinpoint the exact location of chirping crickets (on which the female fly deposits larva).

The Ormia actually has double eardrums, Miles discovered. These eardrums let the fly precisely detect noise direction—a feature lacking in most hearing aids. By studying the fly's ear, Miles developed prototype hearing aids that help wearers focus their hearing and filter ambient noises.

WHAT ARE YOU HEARING FROM NATURE?

"Nature does nothing uselessly."
—Aristotle

how PINECONES
MAKE CLOTHES
smart.

Pinecones aren't just holiday accents for Julian Vincent. He looks to them for ideas.

The University of Bath biomimetics professor wanted to create fabric that adapts to changing temperatures. He started by looking for natural systems that respond to temperature shifts by altering their shape. He discovered several options, but pinecones were the easiest to study.

Vincent found pinecones react to warmer temperatures by opening their scales to disperse seeds. He mimicked their reaction when developing smart fabric. Its weave opens when the climate is warm and shuts tight when it's cold.

ARE YOU WATCHING NATURE'S PERFORMANCES?

"At present there is only a 10 percent overlap between biology and technology in terms of the mechanisms used... there is huge potential."

—Julian Vincent,
BIOMIMETICS PROFESSOR

14

> "A RUT IS A COFFIN
> WITH THE ENDS
> KICKED OUT."
> —*James Hunter*

NOBODY SPOTS IDEAS
in a velvet rut.

In a velvet rut, you're comfortable but unfulfilled. In a drowsy contentment. Sleepwalking. Singing the same old tunes.

An artist's velvet rut is filled with signature styles and rerun projects. A marketer's velvet rut is filled with dusty products and tired plans. A chef's velvet rut is filled with reliable dishes and stale menus.

Chef Rene Margaux hanged himself after twenty-five years at Closserie des Lilas. His suicide note said he could not prepare another onion soup or beef tartare. Murdered by a menu twenty years out of date, wrote one critic.

ARE YOU IN A VELVET RUT WITH NO VIBRANT IDEAS IN SIGHT?

DON'T HANG YOURSELF. *Surprise yourself.*

"You can see that I'm stuck in a velvet rut... sounding like a record that jumps and jumps."

—Billy Nicholls, *Velvet Rut*

"Ease is the greatest enemy of the artist—when you get good at something and just keep cranking it out."

—Chuck Close, ARTIST

BOREDOM IS SO
BORING.

In underdeveloped countries, citizens often complain about hunger. In wealthier countries, citizens often complain about boredom.

Some people even take mood-altering drugs to cure boredom. But being bored is a symptom, not a disease. It's a sign of creative starvation.

Once the brain grasps a concept or masters a task, it wants to know what's next. Sit still and you've got yourself one bored brain.

A mentor once told me, "If you're bored, you're a boring person. With all there is to see and do, there's no excuse for boredom." If you're bored, he said, it's your own damn fault.

"If your everyday life seems poor, don't blame it, blame yourself," Rainer Marie Rilke wrote to a student. "Admit to yourself that you are not enough of a poet to call forth riches."

Don't bargain with boredom. Get up. Get going. Start a project. Call a friend. Call an enemy. Write something down. Tear something up. Build something back.

MAKE SOMETHING BEAUTIFUL.
FIND SOMETHING TRUE.

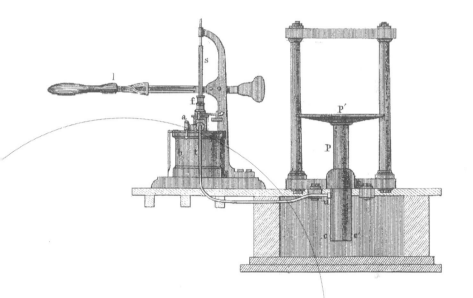

"Nobody is bored when he is trying to make something that is beautiful or to discover something that is true."

—William Inge, PLAYWRIGHT

teach YOUR WAY OUT OF TEDIUM.

Teach a class at a high school or junior college. Teach your hobby at a university's continuing ed program. Teach writing, drawing or photography to inner-city kids. Teach a sport at a recreation center. Teach craft workshops at a nursing home or senior center.

Teach. And spot ideas while you're teaching.

Return to
WHAT REVS YOU.

Steven Soderberg won an Oscar for *Traffic*, then grossed over $150 million dollars with *Ocean's Eleven*. Studios lined up for more big-budget films. Soderberg was heading for a velvet rut.

Seeing it coming, he returned to what brought him to the dance—those recorded-in-our-basement films like *sex, lies and videotape*.

He made *Full Frontal*, a two-million-dollar, indie-type film. To limit expenses, Julia Roberts and fellow cast members did their own makeup and paid for meals and other expenses.

Did *Full Frontal* become a box-office sensation? Hardly. But making the low-budget film helped Soderberg avoid velvet ruts.

REVIEW AN OLD SCHOOL PROJECT. REVISIT AN EARLY ASSIGNMENT IN YOUR CAREER. RECAPTURE PASSIONS AND BASICS LEFT BEHIND.

then again, MAYBE YOU'RE IN A PROJECT YOU NEVER WANT TO RETURN TO.

You've experienced déjà vu, of course, but how about vu deja— that uncomfortable feeling you're experiencing something you never want to think about again.

If you're experiencing vu deja on a project, stop where you are. Start over with a fresh approach.

SHIFT INTO
FOUR-WHEEL DRIVE.

MIX UP YOUR ROUTINE.
Try offbeat restaurants. Read unusual magazines. Take detours to work. Play strange music. Go to unfamiliar films. Attend bizarre lectures. Sign up for whimsical classes. Talk with peculiar people.

CHANGE YOUR ENVIRONMENT.
Switch out artwork. Clean out drawers. Take everything off your work surface—then decide what to discard and replace. Clear shelves—give away useless things, bring in new things. Slap on fresh paint.

BREAK OUT OF ISOLATION.
Lunch with different people. Call on suppliers. Visit workplaces of friends and colleagues. Spend more time in your client's world. Wade into the marketplace.

BREAK OUT OF YOURSELF.
Volunteer at a children's hospital or nursing home. Help a favorite charity solicit donations. Write letters to let professors and mentors know how they helped you. Call lost relatives and rebuild relationships. E-mail an enemy and patch things up.

BREAK OUT OF YOUR BUSINESS.
If you're a designer, look at how writers seek out stories. If you're a writer, look into how actors take on roles. If you're a marketing manager, look at how chefs prepare innovative menus. If you're a photographer, look at how interior designers see a room.

SURPRISE YOURSELF.
Give up what bogs you down. Love something you hate. Appreciate something that annoys you. Look at what you have rather than what you don't. See the whole rather than the holes. Ignore negative thoughts.

PRACTICE NEUROBICS.
Try brain exercises developed by Dr. Lawrence Katz. Sit in different chairs at home and in meetings. Shift your mouse to the other side. Put your watch on the other arm. Brush your teeth with the other hand. Hold your phone to the other ear.

SEEK CHALLENGES.
Volunteer for assignments. Dream up projects. Examine current work and find ways to make it better. Dive into back-burner projects and move them ahead.

V-LINE
your way out.

WHAT RUT ARE YOU IN RIGHT NOW? WRITE
IT IN THE CENTER OF THE V. AT THE TOP OF
THE LEFT STEM, WRITE THE ACTION NEEDED
TO MOVE OUT OF THE RUT. AT THE TOP OF THE
RIGHT STEM, GIVE YOURSELF A DEADLINE.

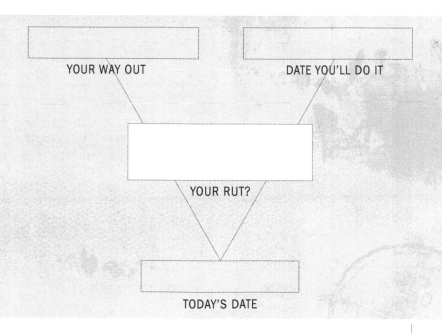

YOUR WAY OUT

DATE YOU'LL DO IT

YOUR RUT?

TODAY'S DATE

TAG TEAM projects.

To avoid ruts and build teams, Starbucks sometimes assigns several designers to the same project. One designer takes over where another leaves off. Such tag teaming added velocity to Starbucks' coffee repackaging project.

"People go back and forth on the same project to the point you're not sure where the original idea came from," says Doug Keyes, senior designer. "It's an addictive process and develops strong links between designers. It also gives an awareness of how ideas flow into other ideas."

WHAT PROJECT CAN YOU TAG TEAM?

wander your
WAY OUT.

Early in his career, cabaret singer Bobby Short enjoyed solid bookings at L.A.'s Café Gala. Good music, good crowds, good money.

But Short soon found himself in a velvet rut. Too comfortable with the same gig night after night. To climb from the rut, he traveled to Europe. There he found stimulation and ideas. He recorded an album for Atlantic Records.

Returning to America, Short signed with New York's prestigious Café Carlyle and in time became a city landmark. He played the White House for four presidents. Earned Grammy nominations. Appeared in movies and TV specials.

And although Short played the Carlyle's posh lounge six nights a week, eight months a year, he avoided velvet ruts by recalling his way out of the first one thirty years earlier.

Short used vacations to get far away from familiar New York surroundings. He saw different people. Tasted different foods. Heard different music.

ARE YOU USING TRAVEL TO PULL OUT OF RUTS?

"We can become blind by see-ing each day as a similar one."

—Paulo Coelho, WRITER

15

"THE WORLD IS A BOOK.
AND IF YOU DON'T TRAVEL,
YOU ONLY READ ONE PAGE."

—*St. Augustine*

GO somewhere.

TRAVEL TO A NEW PLACE.

A new country. A new city. A new street.

Because when you get away, so does your brain. You're bumped from boredom. You notice surroundings. You smell and taste unfamiliar things.

YOU SPOT IDEAS.

On his travels, Chris Bangle, BMW's chief of design, fills notebooks with sketches and observations about fashions, buildings and landscapes.

"Take notes on the world," he says. "There will be a test."

WHERE ARE YOU GOING NEXT?

"Travel is fatal to prejudice, bigotry and narrow-mindedness."
—Mark Twain

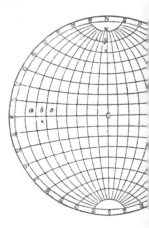

FIND OUT WHAT'S COOKING IN
your world.

When it comes to traveling, chefs are five-star explorers. They pour out of kitchens and onto roads—checking out competitors, talking with suppliers, tasting local dishes.

Jeff Tunks, a Washington, D.C. chef, ventured to Louisiana, spotting ideas for his Cajun-style fish house. For ten days he made the rounds to oyster bars and po' boy joints, crawfish farmers and sausage houses.

Louisville chef Kathy Cary spent time in Barcelona, getting cozy with the city's small-plate concept. Returning to Kentucky, she overhauled menus to showcase her ideas.

And New York chef Mario Batali books eight to ten trips a year, looking for novel ingredients and cultural shifts. On a recent visit to Spain, for example, he added a saffron-scented honey to his cooking arsenal.

ARE YOU TRAVELING NEAR AND FAR TO COLLECT IDEAS?

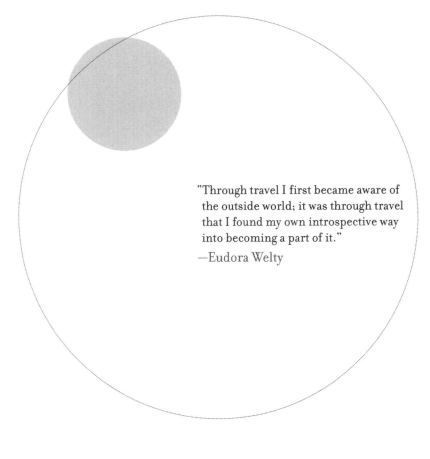

"Through travel I first became aware of the outside world; it was through travel that I found my own introspective way into becoming a part of it."

—Eudora Welty

GO SOMEWHERE *alone.*

It's good to travel with family or friends. But it's easier to spot ideas when traveling alone.

That's because solo traveling allows total focus on the experience, argues travel writer Lea Lane.

"When you're with other people, the possibility of diluting the experience is very high," she says. "I've been at the rim of the Grand Canyon with people discussing their stock portfolios rather than experiencing its beauty."

Julie Taymor traveled alone throughout Indonesia early in her career. Late one night, sitting alone and out of sight under a banyan tree, she watched men perform ritual dances in full costume before a totally empty village square. Ideas she saw there and elsewhere on her travels revealed themselves years later in her creation of *The Lion King*.

"The person who goes alone can start today, but the one who travels with another must wait until that other is ready."

—Henry David Thoreau

TRAVEL *without* PLANS.

NOT ALWAYS, BUT SOMETIMES. AT LEAST FOR A DAY OR WEEKEND.

JUMP IN THE CAR AND GO. STOP WHERE YOU STOP. EAT WHAT YOU EAT. SEE WHAT YOU SEE.

For longer trips, avoid jammed itineraries. Leave time to explore. If a restaurant looks good, try it. If a shop looks inviting, step inside. If there's a hill to climb, a lake to canoe or a park bench to occupy, go for it.

Have conversations with strangers. Check newspapers for local events. Take back roads and side streets. Hop on the wrong train—or even the worst train. The worst trains, notes travel writer Paul Theroux, are the ones that will take you through magical places.

Real travelers don't know where they're going, he says, but tourists don't know where they've been.

BE A TRAVELER.

"The traveler sees what he sees. The tourist sees what he has come to see."

—G.K. Chesterton, writer

SIT DOWN AND
look around.

"Most of my treasured memories of travel are recollections of sitting."

—Robert Thomas Allen, WRITER

Whether your trip is jammed with action or loaded with leisure, remember to take a seat now and then to take it all in. Watch people. Focus on a scene. Listen to accents. Smell the air. Taste fruits. Take notes. Make sketches.

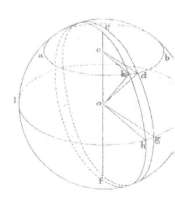

Travel to
DIFFERENT PLACES.

DO YOU LABEL YOURSELF A "BEACH PERSON," "MOUNTAIN PERSON" OR "CITY PERSON"?

FINE, BUT DON'T LET LABELS LIMIT HORIZONS. TRY SOMEWHERE NEW.

Expose senses. "I love traveling where the senses are attacked," says Lisa Greenberg of GJP Advertising. "In India, everything assaults your senses—smells, street posters, crazy monkeys. There's inspiration everywhere."

Eva Maddox of Perkins + Will agrees. "I like exploring unexpected places," she says. "Places where you can see and begin to understand cultural issues and put them in context. This affects my work, life and goals."

SEE THE SIGNS.

For years, Kristy Moore of *Martha Stewart Living* vacationed in cities, spending most of her time in museums and galleries. "But lately my creativity has needed different stimulation," she says.

Moore recently spent three weeks trekking in Patagonia. "With this total change of scenery, I got inspiration from small things," she says. "For example, the primitive signs used to mark trails—a dab of paint or a stack of stones. These markers held their own visual language."

Hallmark's Scott Orazem also heads for remote territory. "I love going to wilderness areas where a person might get eaten," he says, "where there's a possibility of becoming part of the food chain."

GO NEXT DOOR.

Of course, you don't always have to trek across mountains or hike into deep woods to find fresh scenery. Ideas are waiting in that town down the road or shop down the street.

"My latest inspiration came from a piece of coral discovered at a local store I ventured into," says Greenberg.

PLOT YOUR forays.

	PLACES TO GO	DEADLINES FOR GOING
COUNTRY		
CITY		
NATURE AREA		
DAY TRIP		
NEW STREETS		
NEW SHOPS		
GALLERIES		
MUSEUMS		
RESTAURANTS		

"One's destination is never a place but a
new way of seeing things."

—Henry Miller

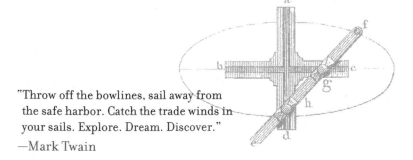

"Throw off the bowlines, sail away from the safe harbor. Catch the trade winds in your sails. Explore. Dream. Discover."

—Mark Twain

WHEN YOU GET AWAY,

get away.

We can't spot new ideas while dealing with old ones. Yet too often we head off on vacations only to let phones and e-mails bring us right back.

I once spoiled a magnificent vacation in the San Juan Islands by calling to check on a sleek, costly magalog we had just rolled out across the country. The news was dismal. Because of faulty glue, magalog pages were falling out like oak leaves on an autumn day.

I spent the rest of the vacation yapping on the phone, fretting over details. In the end, my team back on the mainland solved the problem—just as they would have had I never called in.

I now heed the advice of smart people like Peter Olson, Random House's chief executive. "When I'm gone, I'm gone," he says. "No e-mails. No phone calls. No work-related updates... By the time I return to the office, I usually find myself in a kind of buoyant afterglow."

"When you are everywhere, you are nowhere. When you are somewhere, you are everywhere."

— Rumi,
THIRTEENTH CENTURY
MYSTIC POET

IF YOU'RE AMERICAN,
vacations may seem foreign.

Italians take 42 vacation days a year. The French take 37 days. Germans take 35. And Americans? 13 vacation days a year.

Plus, as columnist Cameron Stracher points out, Americans often don't know what to do with free time. We tend to apply the same diligence to vacations as we bring to jobs, packing them with cell phones, e-mail, voice mail and PDAs. We cram in too many activities, because we're instinctively measuring productivity. We work hard to have fun.

UNDER-PLAN YOUR VACATION.
FORGET EFFICIENCY.

Remember recess.

THIS WEEK,

GIVE YOURSELF FIVE ONE-HOUR VACATIONS.

NO HIGH-TECH CONNECTIONS. NO MUST-DO
TASKS. JUST AN HOUR AWAY FOR RELAXATION
AND EXPLORATION.

VACATION HOUR	DATE / DAY	TIME
#1		
#2		
#3		
#4		
#5		

"An average worker's functioning IQ falls
10 points when distracted by ringing
telephones and incoming e-mails."

—From a Hewlett-Packard
press release

"A vacation is what you take when you can no longer take what you've been taking."
—Earl Wilson, COLUMNIST

IF YOU'RE MIRED, move.

Where do you go when you can't take vacation? When you can't even take a day off? When it's just you and those same old thoughts?

"My quick getaway is Mitchell's, the neighborhood coffeehouse," says Tim Cox, Publix Super Market's creative director. "It's pure community. with a mix of people. Just walking in there inspires me."

Author Robert Louis Stevenson said, "I travel not to go anywhere, but to go. The great affair is to move."

IF YOU'RE STUCK, MOVE.

Move to a nearby park. Move to the library. Move to a hotel lobby, mall or café. Just move.

List three getaways within fifteen minutes of your workplace—retreats for when you're stuck with old ideas:

1.

2.

3.

"If your ship doesn't come in, swim out to it."

—Jonathan Winters,
COMEDIAN

16

WHEN YOU CAN'T GO,
stay put.

AND MAKE THE MOST
OF WHAT YOU'VE GOT.

stay WHERE YOU ARE.

SOMETIMES YOU NEED TO MOVE. SOMETIMES STAY STILL.

Sit and explore—right where you are.

Italian designer Antonio Citterio was enjoying movie night at home with his wife and children. Then he noticed they were seated in a straight line, like passengers on a crowded plane. This gave him the idea for a new family seating concept for B&B Italia, a semi-circle sofa shaped somewhat like a banana.

Because she was pregnant, Spanish designer Patricia Urquiola was paying extra attention to baby dresses. Inspired by the smocking on one little girl's dress, she used the stitching to design her Smock chair for Moroso furniture.

Dan Groggin received a nun's habit from a friend as a joke. He put the habit on an old mannequin and posed it around his New York apartment—washing dishes, vacuuming and performing other household chores.

One day, watching guests laugh at the mannequin, Groggin spotted an idea. Grabbing a pad, he began creating the play *Nunsense*, filled with silly songs and skits.

Nunsense has earned Groggin more than seven million dollars.

WHAT'S HAPPENING RIGHT BEFORE YOUR EYES?

IF YOU CAN'T CHANGE YOUR PLACE,
change your mind.

A trapper sitting outside his Canadian cabin was approached by a land surveyor.

"I've found a mistake in boundary lines," said the surveyor. "I'm here to report your cabin is actually in Montana instead of Canada."

The trapper gave a jubilant yell and danced around the yard.

"You're that happy to be an American?" asked the surveyor.

"No," said the trapper. "I just don't believe I could have endured another one of those Canadian winters."

APPRECIATE CURRENT SURROUNDINGS—
MAYBE THEY'RE BETTER THAN YOU THINK.

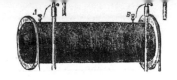

"The world is full of magical things, patiently waiting for our wits to grow sharper."

—Eden Phillpotts,
NOVELIST AND POET

IF LIFE GIVES YOU *limp lettuce,*
MAKE SALAD.

Caesar Cardini's small Tijuana hotel was a famous getaway in the twenties for Hollywood stars looking to escape limelight and Prohibition.

One long holiday weekend the packed hotel ran low on meats. Looking around at the kitchen's ample supply of lettuce, Cardini spotted an idea. He whipped up the recipe for a new salad dressing and pulled together his staff.

"Cart the ingredients to tables and make a ceremony of preparing salads," he told the waiters. "Make guests feel like my Caesar salad is the house specialty."

WORK WITH WHAT YOU HAVE.

Claus Josef Riedel sat at home one night, drinking a favorite wine. On a lark, he decided to pour the bottle's contents into a series of different glasses. Sure enough, each glass slightly altered the wine's taste. Spotting an idea, he created the Riedel set of glasses, each shaped to bring out the best qualities of a particular wine.

DON'T WAIT UNTIL YOUR NEXT TRIP TO LOOK FOR IDEAS.

MAYBE THE ANSWER'S
IN YOUR POCKET.

Erin Whelan, art director at *Real Simple* magazine, was directing a photo shoot for an article about mail-order flowers.

The concept was a floral arrangement with a blank card attached (on which the story's headline would be placed). Good idea, but not jaw-dropping.

The team shot gorgeous arrangements from every angle and began wrapping up. That's when Whelan remembered she needed to mail her rent check before heading home. Removing a postage stamp from her wallet, she spotted an idea.

She stuck the stamp on a prominent tulip in the arrangement, and—eureka—mail-order flowers!

This final shot raised the concept to a higher level—and became the article's opening photo.

SHINE THE KLIEG LIGHTS ON SMALL THINGS NEAR YOU.

see FAMILIAR OBJECTS IN UNFAMILIAR WAYS.

Renoir said when you're preparing to paint a grouping of flowers, first place them in what you feel is the perfect arrangement. Then turn the arrangement around.

black and white.

You're reading this book, so I'll assume you probably enjoy reading.

GOOD. BECAUSE AS PROVENANCE OF INSPIRATION, READING ROCKS.

"I'm amazed when I hear people say they don't read," says Kristy Moore of *Martha Stewart Living*. "Not only are books and magazines filled with smart ideas, but reading develops my thinking process. And smart thinking leads to smart designing."

Scott Orazem, Hallmark's director of design studios, also reads to enhance his creativity.

"I scan the *Wall Street Journal* and *New York Times* every day," he says. "And I read relevant magazines and books. Reading helps me stay in touch with what's going on in lots of fields—and it's a great source of inspiration."

Eva Maddox, principal of Perkins + Will architects, agrees. "I read a lot, and not just architecture-related publications," she says. "I scan *American Scientific*, *Topic* and other periodicals for trends and happenings."

OPEN A BOOK OR MAGAZINE, AND YOU OPEN YOUR MIND.

THREE MAGAZINES AND PAPERS TO READ REGULARLY:

1.

2.

3.

THREE BOOKS TO READ DURING THE NEXT THREE MONTHS:

1.

2.

3.

SPOT NEW IDEAS IN
old ideas.

Several years ago, Rem Koolhaas designed a house for a client who wanted uncluttered living space.

To prototype his idea, the famous architect cut a hole in the core of a wood block. This center space would be the clear living area, with surrounding areas accommodating life's daily accumulations.

Smart concept, but the client decided not to build. End of project—but not the end of an idea.

A few years later, Koolhaas was asked to design Portugal's Casa da Musica concert hall. Out came the block with the empty core.

The open center became the 1,300-seat performance hall. Two walls of the hall are made entirely of glass, suffusing the space with daylight. Rehearsal rooms, recording studios and staff offices wrap around the main hall.

The New York Times called Casa da Musica the most overtly seductive form Koolhaas has ever created. *The Observer* called it ingenious and daringly inventive. London's *Sunday Times* called It a building with an aura of greatness.

NOBODY CALLED IT AN OLD IDEA.

FIND NEW APPLICATIONS FOR REJECTED IDEAS.

"Books help us understand who we are and how to behave. They show us what community and friendship mean; they show us how to live and die... We may notice amazing details during the course of a day but we rarely let ourselves stop and really pay attention. An author makes you notice, makes you pay attention..."

—Anne Lamott, *Bird by Bird*

pull FROM YOUR PAST.

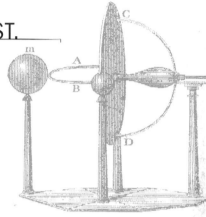

In his plays, Shakespeare often referred to the leather and wool trades. These references most likely came from memories of his father's work as a glover and wool dealer.

Matisse was raised in a family of weavers, and this influence shows up in his work. When painting, he would keep fabrics nearby, grabbing samples when he needed props and inspiration.

Fast-forwarding to today's artists, we have Bob Hurwitz. He runs Nonesuch Records, a boutique label known for creative packaging of its CDs. Hurwitz's passion for packaging stems from his childhood collection of baseball cards.

"Your visual memory retains things for a long time," he says, "whether it's the 1961 Willie Mays cards or the 1965 *Blonde on Blonde* cover or the 2004 Wilco cover."

VISIONS OF
childhood.

Take thirty minutes and a blank sheet of paper. Sketch or write down a half-hour's worth of childhood joys and passions.

WHAT EXCITED YOU?

WHAT DID YOU DRIVE YOUR PARENTS CRAZY OVER?

WHAT TREASURES DID YOU TUCK IN DRAWERS AND BOXES?

WHAT IDEAS IN THESE MEMORIES CAN HELP WITH TODAY'S PROJECTS?

ANTIBIOSIS FILE.

Create a file for rejected ideas. Call it your Farm Team File. Shot But Not Dead File. Better Luck Next Time File.

Or, for a scientific aura, call it your Antibiosis File.

Antibiosis means a restoring to life from a death-like condition, from the Greek *anabioun*, a return to life. That's what happens when we take a comatose idea from one project and apply it to another project.

BLOOD FLOW. OXYGEN. LIFE.

where's your
ANTIBIOSIS FILE?

Keep it where you'll see it.
Thumb through it often.
Check for signs of life.

REGULARLY REVIEW THIS FILE.

seed FILE

Also designate a file to hold inchoate ideas and seeds for possible projects. When you spot an idea with potential, immediately label an empty folder and place it in your Seed File.

Mind and universe abhor vacuums, so backup information will start popping up everywhere—in magazines, on TV, around the Internet, during conversations. Place notes and clips in appropriate folders, seeding your ideas. Before long, you'll have the goods to move forward.

Also create a Seed File on your computer, duplicating the physical file. Use it for screen captures, photos and other digital data.

HOW A LOLLIPOP
BECAME A TOOTHBRUSH.

In 1998, toy maker Hasbro invented a tiny gizmo that transmits sound through teeth and jaw bone. Its engineers imbedded the device in a lollipop that would play a tune in a kid's mouth.

But because of production costs, the lollipop's price point was ten dollars. Parents balked.

The product died, and the idea was filed away. But the story continues.

A few years later, Hasbo marketers wanted to offer a playful toothbrush for kids. They needed a gimmick. Someone looked in the dead idea file, spotted the sound-transmitting gizmo and along came Tooth Tunes, a musical toothbrush.

When pressed against teeth, Tooth Tunes plays a pop song for two minutes—the exact amount of time dentists want kids to brush.

A great idea—and one that began with a DOA idea.

DO YOU HAVE IDEAS SITTING QUIETLY IN A CORNER?

START THE MUSIC.

don't let ideas FIZZLE AWAY.

Mark Constantine once showed Body Shop a fizzling, golf-ball-size item a customer could dissolve in her bath to add aroma. Body Shop rejected the idea, finding the product too unsuitable for its line.

Years later, Constantine started Lush Cosmetics. And he remembered his rejected idea. Today, Lush sells thousands of Bath Bombs daily, and the fizzling product provides forty percent of Lush's sales.

TINKER WITH

old ideas.

You can't always spot ideas just by peeking in old-idea files. Sometimes you need to tinker.

Back in the late 1800s, two sisters, Mildred and Patty Hill, published a little song called "Good Morning to You!" Nobody bought it, so in the files it went.

But the sisters didn't let the idea just sit there. Every now and then, they would pull out the song and tinker with lyrics.

They eventually published the song again, this time with different words. And people ate it up. They sang it to friends. They sang it to family members. They sang it around the world.

And you've probably sung the song within the last month. Because "Happy Birthday to You!" isn't just an idea—it's one of the three most popular songs in the English language.

ALL BECAUSE TWO SISTERS KEPT TINKERING.

LIST THREE IDEAS THAT TINKERING MIGHT REVIVE:

1.

2.

3.

FIND EXTRAORDINARY
IN ORDINARY.

Creative people look at ordinary items and see ways to make them remarkable. L.L. Bean and his boots. Michael Graves and his teapots. Charles and Ray Eames and their chairs.

Recent examples of finding glory in ordinary exist in the restaurant world. Common foods gain uncommon cachet in creative hands. Olive oils. Balsamic vinegars. Farmstead cheeses.

Alice Waters spotted creative seeds in basic foods when she opened Chez Panisse. Her idea was to prepare local produce and meats, serving customers in the style of a small dinner party.

The concept caught fire, and for three decades chefs have mimicked and expanded her concepts.

Alice Waters didn't invent exotic dishes. She just tricked up traditional food that nobody else had taken time to notice.

"The invariable mark of wisdom is to see the miraculous in the common."

—Ralph Waldo Emerson

LIST THREE ORDINARY ITEMS IN YOUR WORLD.

1.

2.

3.

What would make them extraordinary?

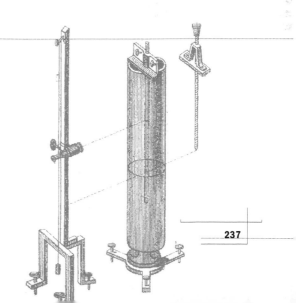

LOOK AT
bits and pieces.

Remember when you took apart that toy as a kid to find out what was inside?

TAKE SOMETHING APART NOW—BUT THIS TIME TO DISCOVER INSIGHTS.

As inferred by deconstruction, you can discover ideas by disassembling things and studying them from different perspectives.

Take apart an annual report. Take apart a branding campaign. Take apart a customer service process. Take apart a product.

Justin Petro of Design Edge uses product dissection to gain insights on how the synergies of materials, manufacturing and design lead to innovation. He calls his dissections "product autopsies." By taking apart products to learn how they live and degrade, Petro makes better choices for his own designs.

WHAT CAN YOU TAKE APART TO SPOT IDEAS?

product teardown: *n.* A detailed product disassembly where all aspects of the item are observed, documented and analyzed from a quality, engineering, design and/or marketing perspective. Teardowns are also used for market and industry perspectives.

What will you dissect?

PRODUCTS:

SERVICES:

MATERIALS:

CAMPAIGNS & EVENTS:

"I'm worried about the kids, Homey. Lisa's becoming very obsessive. This morning I caught her trying to dissect her own raincoat."

—Marge Simpson

17

YOU CAN DO EVERYTHING
WE'VE TALKED ABOUT.

YOU CAN

spot idea
after idea
after idea.

BUT NOT
IF YOU SAY

  "BUT."

or "NO."

or "HOWEVER."

BEFORE PUTTING DOWN THIS BOOK,
put aside three things.

PUT ASIDE JUDGMENT.
Executive coach Marshall Goldsmith has firm advice about receiving ideas from yourself or others: Never start a sentence with "no," "but" or "however."

PUT ASIDE PRECONCEIVED NOTIONS.
"There is a principle which is a bar against all information, which is proof against all arguments and which cannot fail to keep a person in everlasting ignorance," said philosopher Herbert Spencer. "That principle is contempt prior to investigation."

PUT ASIDE FEARS.
"It is not because things are difficult that we do not dare," said Seneca. "It is because we do not dare that things are difficult."

PUT ASIDE WHAT'S STANDING BETWEEN YOU AND CREATIVITY.

Start spotting ideas.

LAST *words.*

"Life is pure adventure, and the sooner we realize that, the quicker we will be able to treat life as art."

—Maya Angelou, POET

"I roamed the countryside searching for answers to things I did not understand."

—Leonardo da Vinci, ARTIST

"My career wasn't one of finding a formula and sticking to it. Instead it was one of exploration."

—Joni Mitchell, SINGER

"I've spent a lot of time asking myself what it means to be an American musician now. It means finding out everything that's going on in America musically. That's why Cajun music and Texas fiddle are interesting."

—Yo-Yo Ma, CELLIST

"I could look at Earnest Hemingway and be inspired to do a whole collection."

—Ralph Lauren, FASHION DESIGNER

"What you see and hear depends a good deal on where you're standing."

—C.S. Lewis, WRITER

"Note-taking is an important aspect of creative endeavor."

—Vera John-Steiner, WRITER

"Anyone who has never made a mistake has never tried anything new."

—Albert Einstein, SCIENTIST

"I travel a lot. I hate having my life disrupted by routine."

—Caskie Stinnett, WRITER

"Like all great travelers, I have seen more than I remember and remember more than I've seen."

— Benjamin Disraeli, BRITISH STATEMAN

"The answer to 'how?' is 'yes.' Say yes to life."

—Dr. Wayne Dyer, PSYCHOLOGIST

"In the age in which we live, the impossible is every day losing ground."

—Anne-Sophie Swetchine, WRITER

"Something hidden. Go and find it. Go and look behind the Ranges—Something lost behind the Ranges. Lost and waiting for you. Go!"

—Rudyard Kipling, WRITER

acknowledgments

THANK YOU, ONE AND ALL.

I offer my thanks and gratitude to the remarkably creative people included in this book. I'm awed by your talents, imagination and generosity.

Most special thanks to my editor, Amy Schell, and to this book's designer, Karla Baker. I wrote the words, but you pulled the book together, shaped it, made it shine. Thanks also to Tricia Waddell for the business arrangements.

To Megan Patrick, who first suggested I write this book, and to all of the other good people and wonderful editors at HOW Magazine—especially Bryn Mooth, Sarah Whitman and Tricia Bateman.

Likewise, my praise to Heather Griffin, HOW Conference program manager, a complete pro at pulling thousands together, even when I'm one of her speakers.

To James Webb Young, who wrote one of the most helpful books about creative thinking in the least number of words.

To Bill Robinson, the first business leader to recognize and reward my creativity.

To my brothers and sister, Bruce, Phil and Diana, who pour wisdom, wit and warmth into our family.

To the clients, associates and team members I've worked with over the years. When I did it right, you almost always deserved the credit. When I did it wrong, you almost always forgave me.

To Gemma Gatti and Hank Richardson, who first gave me the opportunity to teach.

To my students, who keep me thinking and on my toes.

To participants in my seminars and talks. Thanks for coming, thanks for adding energy and thanks for turning off your cell phones.

And, above all, to Hope.
You amaze me.

end notes

16:        Shaun Tan, AATE/ALEA Joint Conference, www.education.tas.gov.au

20:        "Big Fish Story," Hugo Lindren, *New York Times* magazine, 10/26/03

22:        "Masters of Design," *Fast Company*, 6/04

25:        "The Story Behind the Fridge Pack," Jim Lovel, *Atlanta Business Chronicle*, 8/2/02

27:        "The Goods," Brendan I. Koerner, *New York Times*, 3/20/05

33:        "The Sound of Things to Come," Marshall Sella, *New York Times* magazine, 3/23/03

36:        "The Swimsuit Interview," Amy Zipkin, *New York Times*, 1/16/05; "The Guts of a New Machine," Rob Walker, *Net York Times* magazine, 11/30/03

40:        "The Passion Is Mutual," Jack Curry, *New York Times*, 6/16/04

46:        www.ideafinder.com, www.designcrux.netfirms.com

47:        "Electronic Game Maker Lets Kids Do Their Marketing for Them," John Tierney, *New York Times*, 8/5/01

48:        "Present at the Creation," Lars Hoel, NPR Morning Edition, 1/21/02

50:        "Comics Don't Die, They Get Makeovers," Jeffrey Zaslow, *Wall Street Journal*, 4/8/05; "Hot Trends for 2005," Laura Tiffany, Entrepreneur.com, 10/16/04

51:        "New Food Pyramid Sprouts Fresh Ideas for Produce Sellers," Sara Schaefer Munoz, *Wall Street Journal*, 4/05; "Grab Bags," Elizabeth Lee, *Atlanta Journal Constitution*, 5/27/05, American Society of Agricultural Engineers, www.asae.org

52:        "What's Next for Your Living Room," Cheryl Lu-Lien Tan, *Wall Street Journal*, 4/15/05; "Found-Object Furniture Gets Fancy," June Fletcher, *Wall Street Journal*, 6/24/05

54:        www.au.af.mil

55:        www.au.af.mil; credmond/iblog; Animals in Translation, Dr. Temple Grandin

57:        *The Ideas that Conquered the World*, Michael Mandelbaum

58:        "Ad Research Needs Updated Techniques," Deborah Vence, *Marketing News*, 5/15/05; "National Treasure," Joshua Marshall, *New Yorker*, 5/23/05

59:        "How Mirror Neurons Help us to Empathize," Sharon Begley, *Wall Street Journal*, 6/05 "A Career Spent Learning How the Mind Emerges From the Brain," Michael Gazzaniga, *New York Times*, 5/10/05

60:        "The Naked Face," Malcolm Gladwell, *New Yorker*, 8/5/02; "Look Competent, Win Votes," Ellen Warren, *Chicago Tribune*, 6/10/05

61:        *Animals in Translation*, Dr. Temple Grandin; credmond/iblog

68:   "Fast-Food Giants Hunt for New Products," Bruce Horovitz, *USA TODAY*, 7/3/02; "Italian Challenge: Water Everywhere, But Not On the Go," Deborah Ball, *Wall Street Journal* I5/23/05; "Blowing Out Advertising's Walls," Linda Tiischler, *Fast Company*, 6/05

70:   "Are You Listening," Annette Richmond, www.onlineorganizing.com

71:   *LAPC SPIN*, League of American Communications Professionals, 10/05

73:   *Seven Habits of Highly Effective People*, Stephen Covey; www.highgain.com

74:   www.au.af.mil

76:   Roper ASW and *LACP SPIN*, 4/05

80:   "Storytelling, Myra Stark, Saatchi & Saatchi, wwww.saatchikevin.com; "What I Know Now," Keith Hammonds, *Fast Company*, 3/05; *Why I Write*, Will Blythe

81:   "Big Picture Guy," Arundhati Parmar, *Marketing News*, 4/15/05; "Blowing Out Advertising's Walls," Linda Tischler, *Fast Company*, 6/05

86:   www.1000ventures.com

95:   "Let the Customer Drive Design," Jennifer Vilaga, *Fast Company*, 6/05; "Whirlpool Finds Its Cool," Chuck Salter, *Fast Company*, 6/05; "Gross Profits," Rob Walker, *New York Times*, 5/29/05

96:   "Strategy by Design," Iim Brown, *Fast Company*, 6/05; "Get Close to Your Customers," Lucas Conley, *Fast Company*, 8/05

97:   "Ballpark Figure: He's a Hit Pitching Bats to Major League Players," Mark Yost, *Wall Street Journal*, 5/30/05

98:   "Gonzos for the 21st Century," Jack Shafer, *New York Times Book Review* of *The New Journalism*, Robert Boynton, 3/20/05; "Travel," Pamela Paul, *New York Times Book Review* of *My Kind of Place*, Susan Orleans, 12/5/04; "They Come to Praise Brutus," Susan Dominus, *New York Times*, 4/3/05; "Retailer's Rebel Yell," Kimberly Allers, *Fortune*, 10/27/03

99:   "Some Tips from CEOs to Help You Make a Fresh Start," Carol Hymowitz, *Wall Street Journal*, 12/25/04; "The Players," Kevin Conley, *New Yorker*, 7/11/05

101: Body of Truth, Dr. Dan Hill; www.archetypediscoveriesworldwide.com; "The Guts of a New Machine," Rob Walker, *New York Times* magazine, 11/30/03

105: *CBS Sunday Morning*, 1/2/04; "The Play's the Thing," Clive Thompson, *New York Times*, 11/28/04

111: www.clt.cornell.edu

112: "Searching... Beyond Google," Helen Gallagher, The Freelancer, EFA, Inc., 11/05.

end notes

113:     "Designer-Approved," *Fast Company*, 6/05

114:     "Manhattan Takes in a Breath of Mountain Air," Olivia Barker, *USA TODAY*, 6/17/05

120:     "What Lies Beneath," Josh Sims, *Lexus Magazine*, Qtr. 4/04; "The Long-Time Coming Tribute to Underrated Inventions," *Mental Floss*, Jan/Feb/05

123:     "Borrowed Elements in Art," www.vceart.com; "The Best Things in Life Are Free," Seth Godin, *Fast Company*, 6/04

124:     "When de Kooning Was King," Red Groom, *New York Times Book Review* of *De Kooning*, Mark Stevens and Annalyn Swan, 12/12/04

126:     "Off the Canvas and Onto the Big Screen," M.G. Lord, *New York Times*, 12/19/05; "The Guru of Home Décor," Kristina Zimbalist, *TIME* Supplement, Summer/05

129:     "The Nouveaux Totalitarians," Andrea Strong, *New York*, 4/25/05

130:     "All Together Now, James Surowiecki," *New Yorker*, 4/11/05; "Design Inspiration," John Peter, *Automotive Industries*, 12/02; "Trendwatch: Inspired Borrowing," ACNielsen Trends & Insight, us.acnielsen.com

133:     "Standing in the Shadows of Motown," film distributed by Artisan Entertainment; www.cultureby.com

138:     "Philip Johnson: Short on Attention Span, Long on Aesthetics," Ada Louise Huxtable, *Wall Street Journal*, 2/10/05; "Top Marketing Officers Find Getting Together Helps Them Do The Job," Carol Hymowitz, *Wall Street Journal*, 1/11/05

146:     "Rinse and Repeat," Lucas Conley, *Fast Company*, 7/05

150:     "Sound Ensemble," David R. Eltz, *ID*, 10/01

152-153:   Rick Steves, International Travel News, 3/98, www.onebag.com, "The 5 Biggest Parenting Mistakes and How to Correct Them," by Phillip Mountrose, www.en-parent.com, www.shermanleadership.com, Vincent Flanders, www.webpagesthatsuck.com, www.tomheroes.com, "The 12 Biggest Mistakes Directors Make," by Frank Hauser and Russell Reich, Notes on Directing, "Unlucky 7: The top taxpayer mistakes," by Jeff Schnepper, www.moneycentral.msn.com, "10 mistakes dieters make," by Harv and Patricia Haakonson, www.ediets.com, "10 biggest home-buying mistakes," by Pat Curry, bankrate.com, from book, "How to Buy a Home Without Getting Hammered," by David Weekley, Patricia Fripp, www.fripp.com, www.gogirlgo.com.

156:     "Everything in Sight," Calvin Tomkins, *New Yorker*, 5/23/05; www.sptimes.com

159:     *The Courage to Create*, Rollo May

161:     "All You Can Eat," Glen Helfand, *I Am Almost Always Hungry*, Cahan & Associates

164-165:   www.librarybooks4u.com, www.mcsweeneys.net, www.local6.com, www.kab.org, www.longwood.edu, "Lost Property: What Riders Read," by Alec Wilkinson, *The New Yorker,* 10/3/05, www.grocerylists.com]

168: www.poulan.com; "Serendipity: Management by Accident," Reylito A.H. Elbo, *Manila Times,* 5/28/04; www.wildmind.org

170: "Eagle Avenue" www.snopes.com, www.womankindflp.org

172: "The Three Princes of Serendip," Richard Boyle, www.livingheritage.org

173: "The Charity Ball Game," Amy Larocca, *New York,* 5/9/05

176: www.witcombe.sbc.edu; www.mos.org

180: "Kicking Off Her Heels," David Colman, *New York Times,* 5/5/05; "Natural Inspiration," www.bbc.co.uk

182: *Rivers and Tides,* Andy Goldsworthy; "Earthly Delights," Marylin Johnson, *Atlanta Journal Constitution,* 7/17/05

183: www.gogojewelry.com

185: Oregon State University News and Communications Services news release, www.oregon-state.edu; "Ideas Stolen Right From Nature," Rowan Hooper, Wired, www.wired-vig.wired.com, 9/04; American Communications Foundation, www.acfnewssource.org

187: "Ideas Stolen Right From Nature," Rowan Hooper, www.wired-vig.wired.com, 9/04

188: "Pinecone-Inspired Smart Clothes Expand, Contract," James Owen, *National Geographic News,* 10/13/04, news.neationalgeographic.com

192: "Rogov's Ramblings: Boredom in the Kitchen," www.stratsplace.com

193: "Artful Aging," Karen Springen and Sam Seibert, *Newsweek,* 1/17/05

194-195: *Letters to a Young Poet,* Rainer Marie Rilke; www.discoverfrance.net, www.pirnctonol.com

201: allaboutjazz.com

204: "BMW: Driven by Design," Bill Breen, *Fast Company,* 9/02

205: "Roaming Chefs Follow Their Noses," Jerry Shriver, *USA TODAY,* 6/17/05

207: "She's in Love With the Lonesome Road," Gene Sloan, *USA TODAY,* 2/25/05

213: "What I Learned on My Summer Vacation," Christine Canabou, *Fast Company,* 8/02

214: "Getting Away From It All," Cameron Stracher, *Wall Street Journal,* 3/4/05

215: Hewlett-Packard release, as reported in *Fast Company,* 7/05

end notes

220: "Pretty Modern," Karen Klages, *Chicago Tribune*, 5/26/05; "How Silly Nun Jokes Helped: Create a Fortune," Gwendolyn Bounds, *Wall Street Journal*, 2/17/04

223: www.caesar-salad.com; "20 Great Things (to Eat and Drink With)," Alice Rawsthorn, *ID*, Sept/Oct/98

227: "Rem Koolhaas Learns Not to Overthink It," Nicolai Ouroussoff, *New York Times*, 4/10/05; "We Got Rid of the Shoe Box," Deyan Sudjic, *The Observer*, 4/10/05; "Sublime Madness in the New House of Music," Hugh Pearman, *The Sunday Times, London*, 4/10/05

229: "Shakespeare's Leap," Stephen Greenblatt, *New York Times* magazine, 9/12/04; "The Cloths that Filled Matisse's Canvases," J.D. Biersdorfer, *New York Times*, 7/17/05; "Who Cares About Album Covers?" Nick Marino, *Atlanta Journal Constitution*, 7/24/05

233: "Got a Song Stuck in Your Head? Try Brushing," Joseph Pereira, *Wall Street Journal*, 2/25/05

234: "Rinse and Repeat," Lucas Conley, *Fast Company*, 7/05

235: *The People's Almanac*, David Wallechinski and Irving Wallace

236: "Artisanal Items Gain Cachet as Elite Link in Food Chain," John Kessler and Reagan Walker, *Atlanta Journal Constitution*, 7/30/02

238: "Dissection," Justin Petro, Core77, www.core77.com, 2004

244-245: "The Dropout Drops Back In," Martin Johnson, *Wall Street Journal*, 4/13/05; "The Age of Ralph," Bridget Foley, *W*, 8/02; *Notebooks of the Mind*, Vera John-Steiner

index

index

more great titles from SAM HARRISON

IDEASELLING

Successfully pitch your creative ideas
to bosses, clients and other decision makers

A perfect companion to *IdeaSpotting*! Powerful techniques to help you sell your ideas to those with approval power. You'll find road-tested tips from designers, writers, marketers and other creative professionals, plus meaty advice from selling and branding gurus. You'll soon be able to convince those who hold the purse strings that your ideas are worth their dollars.

ISBN: 978-1-60061-669-3
$16.95 pb, 256 p

"This book shows you how to get into the mind of your client and connect with his or her deepest buying motivations."

—Brian Tracy, THE PSYCHOLOGY OF SELLING

ZING!

Five steps and 101 tips for creativity on command

A great little book for big ideas! Use its five-step creative process to generate ideas sizzling with zing—and deliver those ideas in time for deadlines. Punchy, to-the-point messages provide fast examples of creative triumphs, rejuvenating quotes from creative pros, real-world tips and hands-on exercises.

ISBN: 978-0-9744996-3-5
$12.95 pb, 156 p

"Sam Harrison has done a great job in laying out the steps that are bound to increase your creativity."

—Al Ries, THE 22 IMMUTABLE LAWS OF BRANDING